Power with People

Power
with
People

JAMES K. VAN FLEET

Parker Publishing Co., Inc.
West Nyack, N. Y.

PRINTED IN THE UNITED STATES OF AMERICA

B & P—13-686956-4

What This Book
Will Do for You

To be abstract means to be vague and non-specific, or to put it much more bluntly—*to beat around the bush*. And that is precisely the problem I have always encountered every time I have picked up a book that proposed to show me how to achieve success in dealing with people. It has always been too general, too vague, and too abstract.

So in this book I have done away with all abstract and vague generalities when it comes to attaining power with people. You'll find no far-fetched textbook theories of how some introverted psychology professor *thinks people ought to act and what they ought to want*.

This book comes from 25 and more years of dealing with real live people. It was not written in some sequestered sanctuary, but in the active arena of living life. That's why it has no fancy frills—it's all raw meat. And you'll be given methods that really work.

I have been extremely specific and precise as to who, what, when, where, why, how, and the exact techniques you need to use to gain power with people. There are no gimmicks. For instance, in Chapter 1, I come right to the heart of the matter and tell you that the first step in gaining power with people is *not to waste your time cultivating the acquaintance of those people who can't help you succeed, but to—*

Pin-point those people
who can help you become successful

Now there are just no ifs, ands, or buts about that, are there? You see, if you really do want to gain power with people and learn how to control them, you must be quite realistic about it. Then in succeeding chapters, I show you . . .

How to gain information about people who can help you

How to campaign for power

How to get amazing results

How to become your own self-starter

How to gain complete control of people

How to use security and surprise

A power play that never fails

How to develop your follow through

How to build up your own defenses

How to become the greatest in your field

How to develop the touch of the true professional

When you put all these techniques to work for yourself, you'll gain power with people. I know you will, for I've seen it happen time after time with people just like those you'll meet on every page in this book. Just for instance . . .

Arch Spain is a high school teacher who's learned to use these techniques to control his students. Charlie Wright, a high school football coach, uses them to build better football teams in Ottumwa, Iowa.

Imogene Davis has become a successful business woman in Kansas City by practicing these techniques. Even two housewives, Betty Jo Harper and Joyce Caruthers, have learned how to use them to gain power with people.

And then there's Jack Farmer, a retail merchant; Samuel Thorne, a Methodist minister in St. Louis; Pete Ross, an expediter for Zenith; Mike Stone, a shift supervisor in a rubber factory; Lyle Holbrook, a service station operator; Scott Smith, the superintendent of Greene County Schools in Springfield, Missouri; Mrs. Baylor, the "Cookie Lady" from Ames, Iowa; and dozens and dozens more—even my Aunt Martha!

"You'll meet all of them in this book. There's nothing extraordinary about them at all; they're not super-human. You wouldn't find a single genius among them. In fact, they're quite normal people just like you and me.

The only difference is that they already know how to use *Power with People* to get what they want. And when you finish this book—so will you.

James K. Van Fleet

Contents

9

Thirty-three self-starters • 93-104

Pin-point your goal . . . Make a list of everything that needs to be done . . . Put what needs to be done right in front of you . . . Concentrate on the essentials . . . Keep reselling yourself on the benefits you'll gain . . . Give yourself a small part of the job to do . . . Develop a written step-by-step plan . . . Make up some alternate plans . . . Emphasize doing —not doing perfectly . . . Figure out your reasons for putting things off . . . Get your problems down on paper . . . Use your energy for action—not for worrying . . . Learn from others . . . Don't wait for inspiration to strike . . . Work up a self-monitoring system . . . Establish deadlines . . . Make note-taking a habit . . . Insist to yourself that you get started . . . Fight off purposeful forgetting . . . Start off each day with a success experience . . . Clearly distinguish between plans and goals . . . There's a difference between knowing and doing . . . Cultivate your use of time . . . Learn to say "No" . . . Avoid telephone traps . . . Discourage interruptions . . . Listen . . . Do it right now . . . Do it right the first time . . . Do it only once . . . Use all the time you have . . . Anticipate your daily needs.

Points to remember • 104-105

6   HOW TO USE THE FIVE KEYS OF CONTROL   **107**

You'll gain these benefits • 108

Techniques you can use to put this principle to work and gain the benefits • 109

The five keys of control • 110

1

Pin-Point Those People Who Can Help You Become Successful

All of us have at least two major goals in life: *Success* and *Happiness*. And you've taken the first big step toward gaining both of them when you realize that your getting success and happiness depends on other people..

Yes, it's definitely a proven fact. You simply cannot succeed in life without the help of other people. If you want to get ahead in this old world, you must get other people on your side.

You must get them to push for you, stand up for you, cheer for you, vote for you—yes, even fight for you, to stick with you all the way. The best way for you to get ahead is to use your personal power to influence and control—to master and dominate—*certain key people, specific individuals who can help you achieve success in life*. You must find out—*which people can help you the most*.

"It marks an important point in your progress when you realize that other people can help you do a better job than you can do alone," says George T. Vanderhoff, president of Holland Industries, Inc., of Holland, Michigan.

"But you'll really make a giant stride forward in your efforts to succeed when you know who these key individuals are who can really help you become successful.

"Actually, this ought to be your very first goal: *to find out which people can help you most.* Do that, and you'll benefit tremendously by saving time and energy when you *concentrate your efforts only on those people who can help you achieve your goals*. To devote your attention to anyone else is a complete waste of time!"

BENEFITS YOU'LL GAIN

When you pin-point those people who can help you become successful, you'll realize many benefits—that's precisely what I want to tell you about next: the advantages George says you'll gain when you concentrate only on those key individuals who can help you attain your goals and become successful. Here's what they are:

You'll control people

You'll be able to control many people through just a few. You don't need to control the whole human race to be successful. But you can control dozens of people—yes, even hundreds—through just a few key people.

Genghis Khan controlled his vast far-flung empire through certain key people—his loyal tribal chieftains. His was a military empire won by armed conquest. But the same principle of control applies to the economic empire of General Motors. The president of GM is head of an organization that has more than three-quarters of a million employees. He could not possibly control this modern sprawling economic giant without the help of key officers and able administrators.

You'll save time

You'll save time when you concentrate your efforts on the right person. Time is important to all of us. It's a successful salesman's most valuable asset. He'll never waste it by giving his sales pitch to someone who can't make the buying decision. There's a saying among successful salesmen: *Sell the secretary on seeing her boss; sell him on buying your product.*

Ask any business executive what his greatest problem is, and he'll tell you, "Not enough time in a day to get everything done." That's why he carries a briefcase home every night. And if you're like the rest of us—and it doesn't matter whether you're a business executive, a college student, a teacher, or a housewife—you no doubt have the same problem. There just isn't enough time to get everything done. But you can solve most of this problem by *concentrating on the person who can help you do the job.* Don't waste your time on the person who can't help you!

You'll save energy

You'll save energy and effort when you pin-point the pivot man. This is particularly useful to those who work with large groups of people: teachers and preachers; supervisors and foremen; military officers and industrial leaders. But its value isn't limited to those individuals alone. If you work with as few as two other people—and it doesn't matter whether it's on your job or with the finance committee in your church—these techniques can be useful to you, too.

Pivot people are always action people. Their personalities demand action and lots of it. They stagnate in humdrum, routine, monotonous jobs. Learn who the pivot people are in your group; you'll get far better results when you do. Pivot people are especially important to you when you need action and you need it right now. They can help you get that action when and where you most need it. Working under pressure comes naturally to them.

You'll be half-way to success

Find the key person to help you gain your objectives, and you're well over half-way on the road to success. Russell Conwell's lecture,

*Acres of Diamonds,** is probably the most famous speech in the history of the American lecture platform. Although its message will always be inspiring and pertinent, part of its fame came from Dr. Conwell's unique methods.

Dr. Conwell always arrived in a town far ahead of his scheduled speaking time. He would visit the postmaster, the school principal, the mayor, local ministers, prominent businessmen, and other key figures in the town. He won these people to his side long before he stepped to the platform; they helped him win the rest of the people.

You can do the same, whether you're talking to parents at a PTA meeting; speaking to the Thursday night bowling league; attending a meeting of the town council; or addressing the board of directors in a closed conference room. Find the key people and get 'em on your side first; the rest will automatically follow.

You'll become "king"

Find the power behind the throne and you can become king! Key people are often far removed from any official position of authority or responsibility. They will have an aura of influence far out of proportion to their position in the organization. They'll be the unofficial leaders, the pushers, the instigators, the fifth co.umn men, but they'll never be out in front in plain view. Their work all takes place behind the scenes. You must find them; you must know who they are, for you need them on your side to become successful.

TECHNIQUES YOU CAN USE
TO GAIN THE BENEFITS

Find the boss in the house

Every day, a great many decisions, both business and social, are made that require a joint decision of both the husband and wife.

---

* Russell Conwell, *Acres of Diamonds* (Westwood, N.J., Fleming H. Revell Co., 1960).

PTA meetings often boil down to a triangle of father, mother, and teacher. Insurance salesmen and real estate salesmen, as well as car salesmen, face this same problem of getting a husband and wife to see eye to eye on their propositions.

I'm sure you've found yourself in a situation where both the husband and wife must make a decision together. Even though both of them might have to say "Yes," or both of them might have to sign the same document, only one will be the key person—the right target for you to aim at.

The question is—which person is it, and how do you find out? I want to show you how a couple of others run into this same problem, and *how they solve it*, so you'll know how to do it, too.

A salesman finds the real boss in the house   Bob Gallivan, one of the most outstanding life insurance salesmen to come down the pike in a long, long time, and author of *How I Started Earning $50,000 a Year in Sales at the Age of 26* *, has this to say about the role of the woman in making decisions about her husband's life insurance:

"The wife is the key to how much insurance the husband will ultimately buy," Bob says. "On my first visit, I always concentrate on her to confirm that fact. I always question her first, using her given name: 'Mary, what benefits do you expect to get from pensions and social security?' Invariably, Mary has to ask her husband.

"Not only that, I find that most wives have no idea where such vital papers as birth certificates, marriage licenses, wills, insurance policies, and other important documents are kept. Many don't know how to detect tell-tale signs of car trouble; others have no idea of how or where to get the most for their dollar—be it groceries or clothing.

"I do all this to show a wife how helpless she'd be without her husband if something should suddenly happen to him. I insist that she do all the figuring when we get down to the point of how much

---

* Bob Gallivan, *How I Started Earning $50,000 a Year in Sales at the Age of 26* (Englewood Cliffs, N.J., Prentice-Hall, Inc., 1963).

insurance her husband should have. *This is vital!* For the first time in years, perhaps, Mary has become a big part of the financial core of the family.

"When I'm all through, I can guarantee you one thing. The husband may pay the premiums, but the wife bought his policy!"

I'm sure you noticed one thing here in Bob's method of determining the boss in the house. *He, himself, makes the wife the key person! He makes her the boss, at least, for this one small moment of time.* And she takes immediate advantage of the opportunity he's given her; she may never get the chance again!

Not every life insurance salesman can use this approach and make it work, but there's no better one if you can pull it off. It requires skill, experience, and a great deal of tact to use it successfully. I've seen furniture salesmen earn fifteen thousand a year and more by making a backward little house-mouse into a VIP for just a few minutes of time.

Try this new tactic yourself the next time you have to deal with a husband and wife where a joint decision is required. You'll find it'll work wonders for you. Teachers and preachers find it especially useful, too. However, it's not the best approach for selling real estate, as you'll soon find out when you listen to——

A real estate salesman and the husband-wife combination Dale Wells, sales manager for the Fred Myers Company, Des Moines, Iowa, says this about how to handle the married couple in the real estate business:

"A real estate salesman has one of the oddest of all jobs in the selling game. First of all, he has to sell two people on the idea of selling their house. Then he has to sell two more people on the idea of buying it. Altogether, he has to satisfy a minimum of four people, and if the buyers have children, the number of people to be satisfied becomes even greater.

"When I'm trying to get a listing, that is, when I want a couple to let me sell their house for them, I watch the reactions of both of them very carefully. I use a lot of questions to see who will speak up first and to find out which one will turn to the other for an answer.

"If I ask 'How much did you plan on getting for your house?' and John turns to Martha and says, 'What do you think, dear?', I'm pretty sure she's the key to my getting that listing. But I'll follow that one up with more questions. I might ask 'How soon would you be able to move after your house is sold?' Again, if the wife answers, I'm almost dead certain she wears the pants in that house. Here's one that will usually clinch it for me:

" 'Does this window air conditioner stay with the house?' I ask.

" 'Absolutely not!' she snaps. '*I'm* taking it with *us!*'

"Well, no doubt about it now. She's the key to my getting the listing in this case. Papa may bring home the bread, but Mama decides how and when it's going to be eaten! If she signs on the dotted line—so will he.

"I use much the same questioning technique to find the spokesman for the buyers. 'How many bedrooms do you need? Is the living room adequate for you? Isn't this a beautiful family room?' It doesn't take too long to find out who's running that household, either.

"On the average, though, I've found that on the buyers' side, if you can satisfy the husband with the price and the wife with the house, you'll usually close your sale."

Bridegrooms need to know who's boss, too!   Now it could well be that asking a girl's parents for their daughter's hand is completely out-of-date, but getting them to approve of you first will still remove a lot of stones from your marital path.

When I married my "first wife," it was still the custom to introduce the prospective in-laws to each other on some sunny Sunday afternoon so they could size each other up and find out about their religion, their politics, their drinking habits, and their economic and social status.

On just such an occasion when my future in-laws were meeting my parents for the first time, my mother took me aside in her kitchen and said, "You're trying to sell the wrong person, son. Her mother's already sold on you. You don't have to soft-soap her any longer. Now go after her father; he's the key figure. He's the one you need to convince, for he makes the decisions in that house—not her. She just came along for the ride!"

And with that instinctive woman's intuition, my mother was right. He was the key figure and getting his approval was tough. We've been married more than 25 years now, and I'm still working on it. Of course, it might have helped if we'd waited a little longer for his decision back in the beginning and not eloped! (Incidentally, just in case you're wondering, I'm still married to my "first wife." You see, I always introduce her that way. Even after more than 25 years of marriage, it helps keep her on her toes!)

How to find
the key man in groups

Pin-pointing the people who can help you can be a little tougher proposition than finding the key figure in a couple. And the more people there are in the group, the harder you'll have to look to find the key individual. But have patience; it can be done.

Take the average business, for example. Every company always has a few people who wield an influence that has no relationship whatever to their vested authority or their actual position. It's up to you to find out who they are. They can make you or break you whether you like to admit that or not. Here are some of the clues you can use to spot these key people you need on your side.

The pivot man is independent   You can usually spot a pivot man by his need for independent action. Often, this pivot personality or key individual will be a man or woman who has refused a position of leadership or supervision—even though he apparently has all the necessary qualifications—because he doesn't want to be pinned down by official responsibility.

A pivot man solves problems   A pivot man often has a solution for your problem. A great many times the hardest part of solving any problem is simply getting on it. A pivot man can help you get that action when you need it most. He'll often have several suggestions for solving your problems. His ideas are not always the best, but they will help get something moving in a bogged-down situation.

The key man is a creative thinker   A pivot man is usually a creative thinker—a non-conformist. A really creative personality will resist strongly any efforts to restrict and channel his thinking. If his creative urge is strong enough, it will show up in his efforts to get transferred to new jobs, or, at least, to acquire additional knowledge of other departments and other people's work. This may well be your first clue to the presence of a pivot man—a key personality who can help you achieve your goals.

Others rely on him for help   Other members of the group turn to him for advice and help. A supervisor issues an order, turns his back, and walks away. Immediately, the workers gather around one individual. He speaks; they listen. Then they go back to work and carry out the supervisor's order. *But not until they get the unofficial go-ahead from the informal leader of the group!*

When you know him, use the key man to your advantage

Once you've found the key man in your group, you can use him as your unofficial transmitter. You can feel out your group by taking him aside and getting his opinion first. This doesn't make him the boss; it simply gets him on your side. Remember the basic rule: *Find out who the key people are and get 'em on your side first; the rest will automatically follow.*

Above all, don't lock horns with the key man if you're the group's official leader. There's nothing wrong with his influence in the group just as long as he doesn't misuse his power and try to usurp yours. You'll get much further with your group if you work with him and *learn how to use his power with the group by turning it to your own advantage; use it for your own benefit.*

Now let's see how others handle this——

Finding the key figure
is important to industry

"If you're a foreman of a department as I am, or a supervisor, you must know the key people you can depend on," says Bill Kessler, with General Electric's Toledo, Ohio plant. "Then you've got to put them into your key spots—your critical production jobs—so they can watch your danger areas for you.

"I have a man like that on my production line named Hugh Atwood. He can provide the leverage for my department when I need it most. Hugh can make or break the quality image of GE with his soldering iron for he's in a key spot and the movement of the product down the line depends entirely upon him.

"Fortunately for all of us, Hugh has a lot of pride in doing a job well. And he spreads his desire for excellence throughout my entire department. His ability to inspire others along the line to do a better job is worth more to the company than a dozen quality control men checking the end product.

"Yet he's refused promotion time after time. 'Don't want to get all bound up with rules and regulations and red tape the way you do, Bill,' he says. 'You and your management boys can worry about that; I just want to work on turning out a good product for you, Bill.' "

Strange for a man to refuse a promotion? Not at all. Remember, *it's one of the clues to finding that pivot man.* I've known career officers in the service, graduates of West Point, to resign from the army simply because of the command line of red tape that strangles creative thought. The result? The army's losing valuable officers—key people—to civilian business and industry simply because they haven't learned how to identify them and how to handle them. *They haven't learned how to pin-point the people who can help them until it's too late!*

"I'd make a heck of a poor fisherman," Colonel Wayne Zellers told me. "My job is to sell young officers on staying in the army and making it a career. Trouble is, I always let the best ones get away!"

Finding the pivot man is important in business, too "We want to develop our key management people to the maximum," says Lee Summers, vice president in charge of executive development and training with Phillips Petroleum Company in Kansas City, Missouri. "So we shift them from one position to another at definite fixed intervals so they can gain the greatest experience possible and develop a broad and knowledgeable background.

"We do try to locate these key personalities as soon as we can for two reasons: First, the sooner we start developing a man, the better for both of us. Second, we don't want to waste time and money on the wrong individual.

The supervisor who's caught in the middle No doubt about it; most people in business or industry today are in positions that require the utmost tact and diplomacy in working with other people. Even the last man in the management line has to be an expert in human relations.

Take Marvin Powers, for instance. He's a front-line supervisor for the Gold Seal Trailer Company, one of the leading manufacturers in the United States of travel trailers and other recreational vehicles. Marvin is the last link in the management chain. He's the immediate supervisor of the production employee. And he's usually caught right in the middle. If ever anyone needs to know who the key people are who can help him, it's Marvin! Listen to his story as he told it to me:

"I don't know which way to jump," Marvin says. "I have to please everybody: the production superintendent, industrial engineering, quality control, the budgeting and cost accounting people, other department foremen, the men in my own section. But I just can't do it; I can't please them all!

"If I speed up my department's output so that all other production employees in the plant can work at top speed, the incentive goes too high in my own section and the cost accounting people get on my back. Or if my machinery runs too fast, the quality goes down, and the quality control people buck stuff back to me because it isn't done right. When that happens, my own men get their paychecks docked for they get paid only for quality production—not for scrap. Then they blame me for pushing them too hard!

"But if I don't keep up with other departments' demands, then the production superintendent climbs my frame when they complain to him. Course I know he has to keep the plant manager and the sales manager happy, too, as well as the big boys up in Elkhart, Indiana. But all that sure puts me right in the middle. It's just a big wicked cycle!"

I agree with Marvin—but only up to a point. His job does take a lot of know-how to keep everybody happy. But he can simplify his problem by keeping a couple of points in mind:

> 1. *Whom do I have to please to keep my job?*
> 2. *Whom do I have to please to get promoted?*

Now I'm not recommending that Marvin (or you either, if you're caught in similar circumstances) not try to please others, or that you make enemies by purposely stepping on other people's toes. The important point you should remember is this: *Who are the key people to be pleased, in this matter, above all others?* When Marvin answers that question, he'll be well on his way to solving the major part of his problem. And so will you.

Even preachers look for the key figure in the group

"I am always willing that my church should raise my salary," says Samuel Thorne, pastor of the Central Methodist Church in St. Louis, Missouri. "Over the years I've found that the church that pays the largest salary always raises it the easiest. Based on that premise,

I suppose I shouldn't worry about it right now. Still, it's something I've never dared take for granted.

"So when the time comes for the church to consider a salary increase for me, I concentrate my attention on the budget and finance committee to show them how easily we can afford my raise. I personally don't try to sell my whole congregation on the idea; the committee does that for me.

"But I've learned something else, too, through the years. Not all of the key figures are on that budget and finance committee. Keep your eye on that little old lady who says, 'I don't know why the girls always call on me for help and advice; really, I don't. I'm not on any of their committees. Of course, I'm always willing to do what I can to help out. In fact, whenever we're having a church supper, they always call me to ask what they can do!'

"I watch out for her, my friend. She's the one I'll need on my side to get that raise in salary. She's the power behind the throne!"

Colonel Zellers is right—the army does let the best ones get away! David Hall entered the army as a second lieutenant in 1951 having graduated from West Point in the top third of his class. He left the army as a Major in 1963, giving up his rank and his retirement benefits to go to work for an electronics firm in Los Angeles.

I know David personally; he is a good friend of mine. In my opinion, the army let one of its best future generals get away when he left. David has a brilliant mind and the ability to lead people. And he's ambitious. After his day's work with the electronics firm, he goes to school at night. He now has his master's degree, and is looking forward to forming his own company soon.

"I left the army for a lot of reasons, but one of the main ones was that I was never quite sure who I worked for or who had the final say-so on the subject. I simply got tired of trying to obey conflicting orders," David says.

"Theoretically, the chain of command is well established in the army. Yet I've served in outfits where I was never quite sure who I worked for or who was going to make out my efficiency report. The only time they were ever really sure of the chain of command was when someone had goofed and they wanted to pin the 'guilty' part and get the monkey off their own backs! It was sort of a pin-the-tail-on-the-donkey game.

"But I always felt if you want to be successful—you must give your loyalty and your devotion to the man who makes out your fitness report. I still feel that way; that's why I left the army. I got tired of looking for that man.

"*You must know who the key people are in your life.* How else can you hope to succeed? And I don't mean politicking or apple-polishing or some other term they use in the army I'd better not use here, perhaps. But I do mean you should do your level best to please your boss. You should do a decent job for him. You ought to do every-thing in your power to make him look good. *He's the key man in your career.* Out here I know who that man is; in there I was never quite sure!"

And teachers, too!

There's a young high school English teacher named Arch Spain I talk with a lot. In fact, I use him as a sounding board quite often, for he spends a lot of time at our house (not to see me, by the way, but to see my daughter, Teresa). I asked him how important it is for a teacher to locate the key students in his class. Here's what he says about it:

"Students today aren't interested in dead theory or moth-ball morality," he says. "They want to know how a certain subject will help them earn a living and how it will help them get along with people. I always try to impress them with the idea that they are the future of their little town. I tell them that without a doubt this very class has within it a mayor, members of the town council, important business-men and women.

"And since they'll be spending most of their lives together trying to understand each other, they ought to learn how to communicate with each other right now. 'That's what English is for,' I tell them. 'To learn how to communicate; not just to learn how to conjugate verbs!' And to get them to communicate, I ask them for their own ideas and opinions about politics, government, racial problems, morality, church and religion, liquor, dope, and any number of current topics.

"This always brings out fresh ideas and immediate suggestions for improvement from at least two or three key people and soon the rest of the class dives in. From then on I gear everything to the thinking of those few key students, and I have the entire class in the palm of my hand in no time at all. Those few key people do what I want them to do. They step right out in front and the rest follow their lead without question."

Associate with the right people

Not only does it make good sense to pin-point the key people who can help you become successful, it's also wise to associate with them since they can help you get ahead. By the same token, it doesn't make much sense to cultivate the friendship of those who can do nothing for you. Why try to grow a crop of weeds?

Carl T., a good friend of mine, a recovered alcoholic and a member of Alcoholics Anonymous, brings this point out quite well, I think: "If I'd learned earlier in life to associate with the right people rather than a bunch of drunks, I'd never have ended up as an alcoholic," Carl says. "Now I've learned to cultivate the friendship of those people in Alcoholics Anonymous who can help me stay sober.

"After all, I didn't join AA to learn how to dance; I got on the program so I could learn how to get sober and stay sober. I never learned that from any of my drinking buddies!"

POINTS TO REMEMBER

The best way you can get ahead is to use your personal power to influence and control—to master and dominate *certain key people*—

specific individuals who can help you achieve success in life. Do that and you'll gain these benefits:

Benefits you'll gain

1. You'll be able to control many people through just a few.
2. You'll save time by concentrating your efforts on the right person.
3. You'll save energy and effort by pin-pointing the pivot man.
4. When you find the key person to help you gain your objectives, you're over half-way on the road to success.
5. Find the power behind the throne and you'll become king!

How to gain those benefits

1. Find the boss in the house.
2. Sell the boss—not his secretary.
3. Find the key man in groups.
4. Know for sure who you have to please ABOVE ALL OTHERS.
5. Avoid the people who can't help you succeed.

2

How to Become
Your Own Intelligence
Agent in One Easy Lesson

In the first chapter, I showed you how important it is to pin-point those people who can help you become successful. But just to know who they are is not nearly enough.

To gain power with people, you need useful information about them. You need to mount a coordinated, well-planned intelligence effort—it's important that you make up a complete dossier on each individual who can help you. You'll want to know his vulnerable areas which you can later exploit for your own benefit. Therefore, the information recorded in your dossier should be based on your subject's dominant desires or his main points of weakness.

This will take some work, a lot of patience, and plenty of time, but it's not an impossible task for you to do. After all, you don't need to maintain files on hundreds and thousands of individuals to attain power with people.

On the average, you deal with only three kinds of people:

   1. The people who can help you reach your goals and become successful.

2. Those who can harm you or prevent you from attaining your objectives.
3. Those who can neither help you nor harm you.

You need to know everything there is to know about the first two kinds of people so you can use that knowledge about them to your own advantage and for your own benefit. And that's what the rest of this chapter is all about—*How to get that vital information you need about people so you can gain power with them.*

First of all, I thought it would be wise for you to meet a man who's an expert in the intelligence game, a master of the art in the service who's now putting his talents to work in another battlefield—the manufacturing world. Here he is:

"Know what your competitor is going to do. Then you'll be able to beat him to the punch," says Carl Schroeder, an executive with Imperial Coach Corporation, a highly successful Indiana manufacturer of mobile homes, travel trailers, and truck campers. "In the army, I was an intelligence analyst. It was my job to find out *what* the enemy was going to do, *who* or *which* outfit he was going to use to do it, *when, where,* and *how* he was going to mount his effort.

"Then it was my commanding officer's responsibility to take my information and use it to prevent the enemy from accomplishing his mission by beating him to the punch—by attacking him first!

"My job here with Imperial Coach is the same. You see, warfare in business and industry is a fact in our highly competitive free-enterprise economy. Most businessmen are accustomed to such terms as 'fighting for business' and 'battling competition,' but they don't know quite how to go about it.

"That's why the president of Imperial Coach created this new position and hired me—to mount his intelligence effort and to scout both his competition and his potential market. He felt that the basic principles of military intelligence should have a direct application to the profitable operation of his company, but he didn't know how to do it. I brought him that know-how.

"Basically, then, my job boils down to these three fundamentals:

"1. *Finding out what our competition is planning and beating them to it.*

"2. *Finding out what our prospect wants and getting it for him before our competitor does.*

"3. *Polling the right people to get our information.*"

Now let me give you a couple of *specific benefits* you'll enjoy when you gather complete information about the people who can either help you or prevent you from attaining your goals to become successful.

BENEFITS YOU'LL GAIN

Knowledge about people is power when properly used

A pinch-hitter strikes out in the last of the ninth and loses the game. Why? He had no knowledge of what the pitcher was going to throw. But the pitcher knew the batter was a sucker for a high outside pitch, so that's what he threw to him. How did he gain that knowledge? Where did he get that information? His team manager has a complete dossier on every single player in the league. The strengths and weaknesses of every man are recorded in the files. And the pitcher put that knowledge to work to gain power over the batter.

Football teams are scouted the same way. So is big business. That's why new model cars are kept so well hidden until the last moment. The spy in the corporate structure is no longer a myth; he's very much a reality.

Here's another specific example of how knowledge becomes power when properly used. You might keep this technique in mind the next time you get ready to buy a new car, or a new refrigerator, washer, or dryer. It could save you a lot of money——

Turn on the green light—the lady wants a green one! "I love your new model washing machines, but I don't care for the colors.

I wanted one in sea-green, and you don't have that, do you?" you say.

"No ma'am, I don't *seem* to have one in that color," the salesman says, looking around the showroom floor, plainly showing his disappointment at missing a sale. "But let me ask you this. Would you buy this washing machine if I could get it for you in a few days in sea-green?"

"Why, yes, I would," you say, feeling quite safe now. "But I'd want it delivered today, and you don't have one. You said so yourself, and I don't see one anywhere either." You look carefully around the showroom floor again to make absolutely certain there's not a sea-green one hiding out some place.

"Just a moment, please," says the salesman. "Let me check in the back for you." He heads for the storeroom, knowing full well there is a sea-green one back there. And you, my friend, have just bought a new washing machine.

You see, that salesman used his knowledge properly to gain power with you and make a sale. He didn't lie to you at all. He just used the word *seem* and you leaped on it. You thought you were home free. Keep your ears open for that word *seem*, when you're talking with any salesman. It's a red warning flag to watch for.

You, too, can gain the benefit of power with people when you use this technique and others that I'll give to you in just a few moments.

Knowledge is power only when you know it about the right person

Knowledge about someone who can neither help you nor harm you is not power with people. It's not even good intelligence information. It might be interesting, but it's probably nothing more than chatter or idle gossip to clutter up your mind.

You want to gain exact information that can be valuable to you about certain specific people. When you know what your boss wants, what your competitor is doing, what your wife is thinking, what the teacher is planning, what your prospect really wants—you're truly in an enviable position. You have power unlimited. Here's a list of the techniques you can use.

TECHNIQUES YOU CAN USE

1. Find out everything you can about them.
2. Follow the *nine subconscious desires* every person has as a guideline for gathering your information.
3. Always use the *Five W's of Intelligence* to get specific answers.
4. Use the *five points of good interviewing* to draw a person out.

Now let's take up those techniques, one at a time. I also want to show you how others use these techniques to gain power with people.

Find out everything you can about them

You need to know everything you can about the first two kinds of people I mentioned back in the beginning (those who can help you and those who can harm you). When you know everything there is to know about them, you can use that knowledge for your own benefit and to your own advantage. This is not as hard a job to do as it might sound at first. You'll soon find that a dozen or so files might be all you need to gain power with people.

Here's how George Wheeler does it   George is the vice-president and general manager of the Berry Electronics Plant in Wichita, Kansas. George has been promoted. The last time I saw him I was interviewing executives and managerial representatives to gather information for my book on how to inspire others to want to do what you want them to do. Called *How to Use the Dynamics of Motivation,** it's a tool for employee supervision, motivation, and control.

---

* James K. Van Fleet, *How to Use the Dynamics of Motivation* (West Nyack, N.Y., Parker Publishing Co., 1967).

George was the production superintendent then. But he hasn't changed his methods of acquiring information about his employees, even though he's moved up the line. He still keeps an up-to-date dossier on every *key* man in the plant. That's a lot more files than you'll ever have to maintain, without a doubt. But I'd rather let George tell you how he does it:

"I keep a photographic album by department," George says. "I devote one page to each key man in the plant. On that page I keep his photograph, the names of his wife and children—their pictures, too, if I can get them—and all the personal data I can gather up about him; where he lives, what his hobbies are, his strengths, his weaknesses, things like that.

"And I still make it a point to talk to at least five men in the morning when I make my rounds of the plant and five more in the afternoon. By doing that, I'm able to gather more and more information to go in my files. And those files are never complete; they're always growing.

"I don't just talk to people at random. It might look as if I do, and, of course, that's what I want. But you can bet I've picked out my personal targets for the day's conversations well in advance.

"I keep up-to-date data, not only on my department foremen and other key people, but also on certain individuals who'd like to have my job. I always like to keep my flanks protected; I never want to leave myself exposed!"

You might not have to keep as complicated and as intricate a system as George does, but you should post your new data daily. A file that's out of date is worthless to you. In fact, it's misleading. To be of any value at all, it must be kept current.

How to build a dossier from scratch

Henry Thorpe was a technical representative for British Industries, Ltd., back in the thirties. He spent most of that time in Berlin, Germany, for his firm. Henry's hobby was gathering information about Germany's growing military might.

Frustrated because of a World War I wound that had cut short his professional military career, Henry had to content himself at "playing soldier." He did this by keeping himself well-posted on Germany's new Nazi army. He whiled away his leisure hours by compiling complete "Order of Battle" information about German divisions and regiments and their key personnel. Henry fancied himself to be quite a military intelligence expert, and in all truth, he was.

His method of operation? Reading daily newspapers from all over Germany in Berlin's public library. That's all. And just by doing that, Henry was able to take minor bits and pieces of seemingly useless information and build up a complete and comprehensive file on a great part of the German army. For instance, a single item like this one would reveal the exact location of a German battalion:

> Hans Schneider, a Lance Corporal with the 151st Panzer Battalion, is spending a 10 day furlough with his parents. He will return to Dusseldorf on the 18th to rejoin his unit.

Although Mr. Thorpe was not employed by the British Secret Service, he was nevertheless able to help his country tremendously when he returned to England in 1939 with a complete up-to-date "Order of Battle Report" on more than a hundred German divisions.

His information included such major items as unit designation, location, strength, armament, morale, names of commanders and key staff officers. (This last item was especially valuable for European regiments do not rotate commanders and staff officers the way the American army does. There an officer normally stays with his parent unit for his entire length of service. Only promotion or death will move him out.) So accurate was his information that the German High Command later credited England with having more than a hundred clandestine undercover agents in Germany from 1935 to 1939 to gather the information contained in this one report. In fact, after Dunkerque, Henry's files contained the only accurate information on the German army until the underground was organized.

Mr. Thorpe built his entire dossier on the Nazi army from newspaper clippings. You can make yours in a much easier way. You can use intimate person-to-person and face-to-face conversations just as George Wheeler does. To form your own files about your selected subjects, you need only follow certain specific principles I'll give you in the next technique——

THE NINE SUBCONSCIOUS DESIRES

Use the nine subconscious desires every person has as a guideline for gathering your information. Do this, and you'll not waste time gathering useless information. Every bit of intelligence that goes in your files should be relevant to your success in gaining power with people, or it is not intelligence.

What are the nine subconscious desires every person has? Here they are:

1. *Emotional security.*
2. *Recognition of efforts or reassurance of worth.*
3. *Creative outlets.*
4. *A sense of personal power.*
5. *A sense of roots—belonging somewhere.*
6. *Immortality.*
7. *Ego-gratification.*
8. *Love in all its forms.*
9. *New experiences.*

Now it's up to you to find out which one (or more) of these subconscious desires is the most dominant in your subject; which one you'll be able to use to guide and control his actions so you can gain power with him. Find out what he wants *above all else* in life. Do that, and you're in command.

Take the age-old story of Sampson and Delilah, for instance. What were Samson's weak points? Well, he had a number of them, but pride (ego-gratification) and sex (love in all its forms) were the two that finally brought him to his knees. Delilah's weakness was money which to her represented emotional security. Cold hard cash gave her (and many other people) a sense of safety and security that nothing else could do.

"And the lords of the Philistines said unto her . . . we will give thee every one of us eleven hundred pieces of silver." And Delilah accepted. Quite a tidy little sum of money for a girl—even in these days of inflation!

Sex and money are the two oldest tools in the spy business; they're still being used quite effectively today, too. And some people think that professional soldiering is the oldest profession in the world. How wrong they are—it's only the second oldest!

Corporations use the nine subconscious desires

Even big corporations use these nine subconscious desires to sell their products. They are very sophisticated about the procedure; they call it the *depth approach*. General Motors uses it to sell cars; so does Ford. And Chrysler, too. Then there's Westinghouse, General Electric, Zenith, RCA, Marlboro, General Foods, Mogen David Wine, and a host of others too numerous to mention, who sell their products by using the depth approach to reach a man's subconscious desires.

What is the depth approach?   The depth approach is a technique designed to reach a person's deep or subconscious mind so they can influence and control the choices he makes in his subconscious mind that are to your benefit and to your advantage. It allows the user to gain power with people.

I know a lot of people just like you and me who use it, too. Just for instance—teachers and preachers, insurance and real estate salesmen, fathers and mothers, doctors and lawyers, businessmen and executives who use the depth approach to gain power with people by controlling them through their subconscious needs and desires. Even my Aunt Martha uses it!

The depth approach can be used to make more money   That, of course, is the main reason big business and industry use the depth approach to reach one or more of a person's deep subconscious desires—*to make more money.* That's why the big names like General Motors, Ford, Chrysler, Westinghouse, Zenith, RCA, General Foods, etc., all use it. They appeal to one or more of the buyer's nine deep subconscious desires so they can sell more and more of their product.

Soap manufacturers don't sell soap anymore—they sell soft hands and beauty. (As my youngest son says—they never say a word about getting the dishes clean!) Cosmetic makers don't sell lanolin—they sell hope. You don't buy oranges and apples—you buy health and vitality. Nor do you just buy transportation when you buy a car—you buy prestige.

Now let me give you some concrete examples of how others use a man's subconscious desires to benefit themselves.

How big business sells emotional security

For example, the sale of home freezers skyrocketed after World War II. Why? People needed *emotional security;* a freezer full of food, after the lean years of food rationing and meat scarcity, gave it to them. Food in the house in abundance represented *warmth, security, and safety* to them.

When so many of us live within five minutes or so of a shopping center, home freezers make little sense in view of their high initial cost, the increased electric bill, and the fact we already have quite a hefty freezing compartment in our refrigerators. But when a person wants *emotional security,* all these disadvantages give way to that subconscious desire of his. (Yes, I have one, too!)

One of the very best approaches to reach the subconscious desire for emotional security is the Allstate Insurance Company's closing statement in its TV commercials, *"You're in good hands with Allstate."* The effectiveness of that statement is given an extra plus with those two strong hands cupped together on your TV screen.

Drug manufacturers sell reassurance of worth

Even doctors are susceptible to the subconscious desire for a *reassurance of worth* or *recognition of efforts.* The smart drug houses recognize this, too. They will make no claim whatever for the good results of their products to the eventual user—the doctor's patients. Instead, they seek to build up the doctor's image as the *all wise seer and healer of the sick*. They put him in the limelight to take the bows, even though their drugs got the patient well!

A housewife needs a creative outlet—General Foods obliges her General Foods found that a cake mix to which the housewife added only water would not sell. But a cake mix that asked her to "add two eggs and one cup of milk" did. More trouble for her to make? Yes. Then why did she buy the more troublesome cake mix? Because she needed to fulfill her need for a creative outlet. Adding only water gave her no chance for *creative expression.*

Selling a sense of power

A person's subconscious need for more *personal power* has been used for years in the Detroit horsepower race. Sears, Roebuck now advertises a battery with the phrase, *"Naked Power!"* Boat manufacturers also use it to their advantage, as do makers of lawn mowers and household power tools.

People need a sense of roots— a sense of belonging

Real estate salesmen who try to sell houses without selling *a sense of roots* aren't using the biggest sales tool they have in their kit. That's the primary reason people buy homes instead of renting apartments or town-houses—to put down *a sense of roots* and to gain *a feeling of belonging somewhere.*

The Mogen David Wine people used it to come from obscurity to one of the best known wine makers in the world with an annual advertising budget now figured in the millions! How? Not by selling their wines, but *by appealing to the buyer's need for a sense of roots!* They sold nostalgia for the good old days—Grandma's country kitchen, fireplace and all, even to people who never had a Grandma!

The double-barreled shotgun

Vanity publishers use two subconscious desires when they sell an author on the idea of paying for the publication of his book: *ego-gratification* and *immortality*. Authors who can't get published by a regular publishing house have been known to mortgage all but their souls to get their books into deathless print!

I'm not going to cover each subconscious desire in this chapter with specific examples. Now that you know how it works, you can start finding your own. And keep your eyes and ears open when you're at work. It won't be long before you can define these same areas of weakness, some more prominent than others, in your associates, your employees, your boss, your friends, your customers. And these weaknesses are to be recorded in each dossier.

Once you find which of these desires is an individual's greatest need—and therefore, his greatest weakness—you can start hammering away at it. Sooner or later, you'll be in control, just as Betty Jo Harper is with her husband——

How to catch and hold a man   "I learned how to control a man from my mother-in-law," says Betty Jo. "Shortly after we were married, my husband and I had the usual disenchantment most young couples encounter, and since my own mother had died in my early childhood, I had to turn to my mother-in-law for help. Thank God for her understanding; she helped me plot against her own son!

" 'The only way to control a man so he doesn't know that you're doing it is to go through his subconscious,' she told me. 'Women 'round the world use a variety of tactics to hold their men. Take a tip from each of the more successful ones.'

"In brief, she told me to 'be to your husband all these: a Chinese cook in the kitchen, a Japanese wife in the bath, a French mistress in the bedroom, an English hostess in the living room. Do that,' she said, 'and your busband will be true to you all his life!'

"And my friend, that's so true. I have 30 years of marriage, four children, and seven grandchildren to prove it. Maybe he looked at another woman now and then, but only with his left eye. He kept the right one on me all the time!"

A person's subconscious desires can change   This is why you have to keep your files up-to-date all the time. A person's subconscious desires are always in a state of flux. Just for instance, take a look at Jim Winters:

"I spent a little over 30 years in service in the army," says Jim, "and when I retired, I wanted a permanent home more than anything else in all the world. *I wanted to put down roots; I wanted to belong somewhere.* I guess that house gave me a sense of security I'd never had before. Brother, that real estate salesman didn't sell me a house. He didn't have to—I took it away from him!

"But after I'd been there a couple of years, I sold it and bought a travel trailer. I needed *new experiences* far more than I needed to put down roots. And I was sick and tired of looking at the same old scenery day after day.

"Now my wife and I spend our winters in Mexico, our summers in Washington and Oregon, and the fall and spring in Arizona, New Mexico, and southern California. Why I've even written a few articles for some of the travel magazines to pick up some extra pocket money!" (Jim is filling his need for a *creative outlet* with that last one, though he probably doesn't even realize it himself.)

HOW TO BE YOUR OWN INTELLIGENCE AGENT

Please keep one thought in mind here. Although a lot of the examples I've shown you were people actively engaged in achieving their goals of power with other people, they were using their previously gathered intelligence information to do so. In this chapter we're interested only in learning how to gather the information that will be helpful to you. Here I want to show you how you can be your own intelligence agent by gathering information about a person's deep subconscious needs and desires. In a later chapter I'll show you how to fulfill those subconscious desires. Together these two chapters will give you the great secret of achieving power with people, which is— *Finding out what they want,* and *Helping them get it.*

The Five W's of Intelligence

Always use the Five W's of Intelligence to get specific answers. To gather reliable information about your subject, you must talk with him. You must question him so he will talk; then you must listen to his answers. Be specific in your questioning techniques to bring out the answers you need that will help you. You can do that if you use the Five W's of Intelligence to ask—*Who? What? When? Where? Why?* and *How?*

Make it a point to gather several items of information daily. Then do your homework and record them each night in his dossier. Remember, no file is ever completed. A man's desires are constantly changing, as are his opinions and his attitudes. Look at Jim Winters's comments again.

Five steps to good interviewing   Use the five points of good interviewing to draw a person out. Getting a man to talk about himself and what he wants out of life more than anything else is easy if you use the five specific techniques of interviewing along with the Five W's of Intelligence. Here's all you have to do:

1. Become genuinely interested in other people.
2. Be a good listener.
3. Encourage others to talk about themselves.
4. Talk in terms of the other man's interests—what he wants.
5. Make the other person feel important—and do it sincerely.

How to become genuinely interested
in other people

"I have no problem whatever in becoming genuinely interested in other people," says Lawrence Lee, a department foreman with the 3M Company. "Why? Well, actually because I'm interested in what he can do for me; and that has to make me interested in him.

"But I concentrate on my goal—not on whether I like a man or not. My goal is to get information out of him—information that will be worthwhile and valuable to me. As long as I remember that my being genuinely interested in him can be beneficial to me, I'm in good shape.

"In planning my interviews, I fix a definite objective in my mind. It's always best for me to fix my mind on a specific target rather than the individual. Once I know where I'm going and what I'm after, then it's full steam ahead. That's why I'd rather pick a concrete goal first—then the person to help me reach that goal.

"You see, when you do that, certain people will come to your attention automatically. And you can't achieve your objective of getting the information that you want without talking to those people. So you can't help but take an active and genuine interest in other people to get what you want. Actually, you have no other choice!"

How to be a good listener

"The ability to listen is one of God's rarest gifts to a woman," says Joyce Caruthers, a smiling happy-faced mother of three from Joplin, Missouri. "When my husband comes home at night, I'd love to tell him how harassing and nerve-wracking my day has been—but I don't. Instead, I listen to his problems.

"And I ask such questions as 'And what did you do then? And what did he say to that? What was his opinion after that?' My questions give Harry a good chance to unload and blow off steam at home where it's safe and where it won't hurt him. But I'll bet his boss would give anything to pick my brains and find out what I know!"

If you're having trouble getting your husband to take you out to dinner or to a movie now and then, try Joyce's system. It'll work wonders for you. If your husband can't unload his problems on you at home, he'll find someone at the nearest bar to tell his troubles to.

How to encourage others to talk about themselves

It might be hard for you to keep quiet, but getting another person to *talk about himself* is the easiest job in the world. Just ask a few questions, show some real interest and listen, and you'll learn plenty to go into his dossier that night. Do as Joyce Caruthers does, or develop your own techniques. Or you might try Marion Hunt's approach. Here's what she does:

"A lot of girls think that if you're going to be popular with the fellows and get a lot of dates, you've got to go all the way with him. That's not true at all," Marion says. "My phone is always ringing and I have a lot more offers for a date than I can accept. What's my secret? Simple, really. I use only four words and I have never had to sit at home alone yet. All I say to a man is—'*Tell me about yourself!*' And he does—and loves it, too!"

How to talk in terms of the other man's interests

Here, it's a matter of finding out which of his subconscious desires is the most dominant. Find out what he wants more than anything else in life. A lot of times he doesn't even realize himself what his primary desire is. In fact, amazingly, often you'll be able to help him discover for himself, for the first time, what he really needs to be happy and contented with life.

Frank Bettger, one of America's top salesmen of all time, and author of *How I Raised Myself from Failure to Success in Selling,**

---

* Frank Bettger, *How I Raised Myself from Failure to Success in Selling* (Englewood Cliffs, N.J., Prentice-Hall, Inc., 1958).

says this:

"When you show a man what he wants, he'll move heaven and earth to get it. This universal law is of such paramount importance that it takes precedence over all other laws of human relations. It always has been and always will be the most important. Yes, it looms up as Rule Number One over all other rules in civilization."

If a man'll move heaven and earth to get what he wants, and if you're the person who can offer him what he wants, then you can't help but benefit, can you? So always talk in terms of another man's interests. Remember, when he gets what he wants, you should get what you want, too. If you don't, you're using the wrong technique!

The last rule of successful interviewing is to——

Make the other person feel important—and do it sincerely!

"I am proud of you" are five of the most precious words you can ever use to make another person feel important. You can use them any time of the day on your boss, your employees, your friends, your husband, your wife, or your children. They will work seeming miracles for you.

"I've never found any better words to use with my players than *I'm proud of you!"* says Charlie Wright, high school football coach in Ottumwa, Iowa. "When a boy makes a touchdown or makes a terrific block or intercepts a pass, just to say, 'That's wonderful, Bill,' doesn't fetch it. But if you put your hands on his shoulders, look him square in the eyes, and say, *I'm proud of you,* Bill!'—man, he'll play his heart out for you to make you look good!"

What about your enemies?   When you're building your dossier on those people who could harm you, do so with the viewpoint of turning them into friends. If you can't, at least you'll know their intentions ahead of time. You can take the appropriate protective measures, just as George Wheeler does.

POINTS TO REMEMBER

To gather useful information about people, you need to mount a coordinated, well-planned intelligence effort. Normally, you deal with only three different kinds of people—only the first two are important in building your files—

1. People who can help you reach your goals and become successful.
2. People who can harm you or prevent you from reaching your objectives.
3. Those who can neither help you nor harm you.

No matter whether it's competition in business, winning a wife, or holding a husband, gathering intelligence information so you can gain power with people boils down to these three basic fundamentals:

1. Finding out what your competitor is planning and beating him to it.
2. Finding out what your prospect wants and getting it for him before your competitor does.
3. Polling the right people to get your information.

Again, the nine subconscious desires

1. Emotional security.	6. Immortality.
2. Recognition of efforts.	7. Ego-gratification.
3. Creative outlets.	8. Love in all its forms.
4. A sense of power.	9. New experiences.
5. A sense of roots.	

And, the Five W's of Intelligence

1. Who?	4. Where?
2. What?	5. Why?
3. When?	6. How?

Remember the five points of good interviewing

1. Become genuinely interested in other people.
2. Be a good listener.
3. Encourage others to talk about themselves.
4. Talk in terms of the other man's interests—what he wants.
5. Make the other person feel important—and do it sincerely.

Use these techniques and you can gather intelligence information that will enable you to gain power with people.

3

How to Plan
a Successful Campaign
for Power with People

Once you've picked out the people who can help you attain your objectives in life so you can become successful, and after you've gathered enough intelligence information about them to know what their most dominant desires are, what's your next logical move?

Well, your next step should be to formulate your plans so you'll be able to get what you most want out of life—to reach your own particular goals—to achieve success. And getting what you want, attaining your goals, becoming successful, means using the help of other people.

In other words, if you want to succeed, you need three big factors:

1. A *GOAL*.
2. A *PLAN* to reach that goal.
3. *PEOPLE* to help you put your plan into effect so you can reach your goal.

I'm sure you already know what your goal is. And by knowing your goal, you'll also know which people in your life are necessary to help you achieve that goal. So I'm going to devote this chapter to the one unknown factor—*your plan for reaching that goal.*

But I'd like to ask you not to forget this one big important point: *You cannot accomplish anything in life without the help of other people.* A successful writer becomes successful only because people buy his books. A famous artist becomes famous only because people made him so. Even Mr. B. L. Mellinger, Jr., of Los Angeles, California, who's known as the "mail-order king," depends on people he's never met to buy his products. How else could he have gained that title?

I'm going to give you a skeleton plan, an outline you can apply to fit your own individual circumstances, be it your desire to gain more sales for your company; win over a business competitor; be a better schoolteacher or a better wife and mother; or get your own programs and policies put into effect at your country club. Before we get into the details of planning, though, let's first take a look at——

SOME OF THE BENEFITS YOU'LL GAIN WHEN YOU PLAN

You'll gain purpose and direction

Planning your campaign for power with people will give you both purpose and direction. Planning for power with people starts out with getting the right job. Getting a job today is not hard at all. Anyone can get a job of some sort if he really wants to work. But is that what you really want; just any old job? One of the quickest ways to determine whether you can use your specific job as a springboard to success or not is to ask yourself these two questions: "Will this job give me what I really want out of life? Will it offer me a chance to go up the ladder and gain power with people?" If it will not, chances are it's not the right job for you.

If you plan your career based on those two simple questions, you'll get out of a dead-end job, if you're in it. If you're not in it yet, you can avoid it. When you add purpose and direction to your life, it makes it well worth living. Each new day is exciting and worth while.

You'll decide
what you want to do and be

Establishing your goals will help you decide what you want to do and be. Set a definite goal for yourself and have a specific plan, to include a definite time limit, to reach it. Don't use such vague generalities as "I'll be the sales manager some day—wealthy by middle age—retire sometime before I'm 65." These are death-traps; they won't get the job done for you. Know exactly where you want to go, what you want to be, and what you want to do. Then you'll be able to determine which people you need on your side to help you get there.

Planning your career will force you to decide what you want most. Then you can rule your circumstances instead of letting your circumstances rule you. This also works in reverse. Knowing what you want will force you to make up your own plan of action to get it.

You'll achieve
perseverance and success

Planning your campaign for power with people will give you perseverance and a determination to succeed. A war is won battle by battle—campaign by campaign—one after the other. A ladder is climbed one rung at a time. Nearly everything in life is done little by little. And so it should be in your own planning for success—for power with people. Give yourself some short-range goals and you'll increase your determination to go on to the next one as each intermediate goal is reached.

There's no obstacle conceived by the mind of one man that cannot be overcome by the mind of another man who's filled with perseverance and determination to succeed. The only obstacle that can prevent you from succeeding will be in your own mind.

And now for your actual planning. Your plan should be able to bring you success in these five vital areas of your life—1. *Social*, 2. *Spiritual*, 3. *Mental*, 4. *Family*, and 5. *Financial*.

A PLAN OF ACTION FOR SUCCESS

And your plan will, if you tailor it after the skeleton outline below. This plan of action can be the chart that gives direction to your dreams. It can help you to succeed and to get what you want out of life. Here it is:

1. Establish your short-range goals and your long-range goals.
2. Set up your tangible and your intangible goals.
3. Learn to recognize obstacles, road-blocks, and problems. Get rid of them, go around them, or solve them.
4. Use your initiative, your imagination, and your ingenuity.
5. Determine where you are now in relation to your goals and measure your progress on a regular basis.
6. Set realistic and reasonable dates for reaching each one of your goals.
7. Picture in your mind the rewards that will be yours when you reach your goals.

And now let's cover these seven techniques one at a time, in detail.

Establish your short-range and your long-range goals

Sometimes it's hard to see or understand the exact difference between your long-range goals and your short-range or your intermediate goals. Actually, your long-range goals should be your ultimate aims, your final goals, in the five vital areas of your life. Your short-range or your intermediate goals will be those little victories that act as road markers or milestones on your way to those long-range goals.

I can best show you that difference by telling you about Imogene Davis who owns her own stylish ladies dress shop:

"I started out working in the ladieswear department in Barth's in Kansas City," Imogene says. "I was a sales girl, but I didn't want to be just a clerk for the rest of my life. So I immediately gave myself some intermediate goals and one final long-range objective.

"My first intermediate goal was to learn everything that I could about my job as a sales girl and do it better than anyone else. My next one was to become the department manager. Third, I wanted to be the buyer for all women's wear for the entire store. My last intermediate goal was to save enough money from my salary so the bank and I could open my own shop.

"That was my fourth and final goal: my own business, and I reached it when I opened my own store here in the Blue Ridge Mall. By the way, the bank is no longer my partner, at least, for the time being. They were also a short-range intermediate goal. I needed them only to reach my final objective.

"However, I'm going to take them back into partnership for a little while next month. You see, I'm opening another shop over in North Kansas City for I've now given myself another 'final' goal: a chain of dress shops!"

You, too, can follow Imogene's example yourself if you'll just follow these four points:

1. *Learn all there is to know about your present job and do it better than anyone else can do it.*
2. *Win promotion to the next higher position and repeat step one.*
3. *Save enough money out of your current earnings so you* (and the bank) *can set up your own business.*
4. *Locate and buy your own business—or create one—that will satisfy your final goal.*

Don't forget. You need power with people every step of the way to your final goal. I've never met anyone yet who could run a successful business without the help of people—real live customers!

Set up your tangible
and your intangible goals

I think it's quite easy to fix tangible goals in your mind—a bigger home, a second car, that sort of thing. The only danger with fixing only materialistic, tangible goals in your mind is a tendency to try and keep up with the Joneses. And that can lead to ulcers and more ulcers if you have only tangible goals. So give yourself some intangible goals, too. They'll help to temper and make your materialistic drives much easier to live with. Let me say it this way. . . .

Tangible goals are most often defined as *prestige symbols that represent success to most people.* Intangible goals could be creative accomplishments of some sort that have nothing whatever to do with money. However, the two goals, tangible and intangible, can often be tied together like this: *Striving to be successful can bring self-satisfaction, fulfillment, and happiness—intangible goals—as well as material wealth—tangible goals.* Or as Earl Nightingale, the famous Chicago radio announcer, so aptly put it once, "Success is not the result of making money; making money is the result of success."

To reach both your tangible and your intangible goals, you might want to follow the pattern contained in——

Mr. Meyer's Million-Dollar Success Plan   Mr. Paul Meyer is the founder and president of Success Motivation Institute of Waco, Texas. His organization is the world's foremost producer of personal motivation, leadership development, and sales training recorded courses.

Mr. Meyer, who made his first million by the time he was only 27 selling insurance, used this very same plan to become a millionaire. Incidentally, he didn't inherit his fortune, either; he made it. When he was only 17, he was picking prunes for a living! Here's his formula for success in his own words:

"I believe in what I call the *Million-Dollar Success Plan,* which consists of five major points," Mr. Meyer says. "It is my prescription for success.

"a. *Crystallize your thinking.*

"Determine the specific goals you want to achieve. Then dedicate yourself to their attainment, with unswerving singleness of purpose and the zeal of a crusader.

"b. *Develop a plan for achieving your goal, and a deadline for its achievement.*

"Plan your progress carefully—hour by hour, day by day, month by month. Organized activity and maintained enthusiasm are the backbone of your power.

"c. *Develop a sincere desire for the things you want in life.*

"A burning desire is the greatest motivator of every human action. The desire for success implants 'success consciousness' which, in turn, creates a vigorous and ever-increasing 'habit of success.'

"d. *Develop supreme confidence in yourself and in your own abilities.*

"Enter every activity without giving mental recognition to the possibility of defeat. Concentrate on your strengths, instead of your weaknesses . . . on your powers, instead of your problems.

"e. *Develop a dogged determination to follow through on your plan.*

"To do this, you must disregard completely obstacles, criticism, or what other people say, think or do. Construct your determination with sustained effort, controlled attention, and concentrated energy. Opportunities never come to those who wait. They are captured by those who dare to attack!"

Learn to recognize roadblocks . . .

Learn to recognize obstacles, roadblocks, and problems. Get rid of them, go around them, or solve them.

"It seems to me I spend more than half my time in unproductive business conferences trying to answer my subordinates' questions about their problems," Hugh Roberts, production superintendent with Dayton Rubber and Plastics Corporation, complained to me. "I've got enough problems of my own to solve; I don't need their problems, too.

I need more answers—not more questions! Can you outline a method for me, Jim, that will help all of us to make decisions; to find answers to our own problems?"

"I sure can, Hugh," I said, and I did. That was over two years ago. Yesterday at lunch Hugh told me he was still using the problem-solving technique I'd outlined for him. "I didn't even change a comma or a period, Jim," he said. "I didn't have to!"

So I figured if my problem-solving technique was that good for Hugh, you would like it, too, so here goes:

You must become an expert in solving problems   If you want to gain power with people, you'll need to become an expert in solving problems—*especially theirs.* You must step out and take the lead. Solve those problems while they're small; don't give them a chance to grow.

If you're an executive, you'll be required to make sound and timely decisions about your own business and your own employees. If you're a minister, you'll have to solve problems and make decisions time and again for members of your congregation. If you're a teacher, your students will come to you for help every day of the week. No matter who you are or what you do, if you can become an expert in solving people's problems, you'll gain power with them.

In solving problems, you'll often find you cannot rely upon past experiences or present observations as infallible guides to arrive at a sound and sensible decision. *Yesterday's solution may not always fit today's problem.*

So it becomes essential that you follow a definite and logical step-by-step procedure which can be used to solve any of your problems in an orderly and analytical manner. This is especially important if you're faced with an inflexible time deadline.

The problem-solving process   There are three general steps to follow in the problem-solving process. They are——

1. *Recognize the problem.*

2. *Make an estimate of the situation.*

3. *Take the appropriate action.*

And now, in detail. . . .

1. RECOGNIZE THE PROBLEM.

What is a problem anyway? It is any situation, or any set of circumstances, that prevents you from reaching a specific goal or objective, or from doing a certain thing you desire to do.

You must clearly define and determine the limits of your problem. What are its boundaries? Its limitations? Its exact nature? You must find all the pertinent details and gather up all the facts bearing on the case. Once you know exactly what your problem is, you're ready to——

2. MAKE AN ESTIMATE OF THE SITUATION, BY . . .

A. *Determining the exact cause.* Who is involved? What are the exact circumstances? When and where did it happen? To be sure that you cover the entire field of possibilities in determining the exact cause of your problem, run it through this gauntlet——

(1) WHO is involved?

(2) WHAT are the exact circumstances—the precise conditions?

(3) WHEN did this problem first appear?

(4) WHERE exactly did it happen?

(5) WHY (HOW) did it happen?

B. *Determining all possible solutions.* After you've determined the cause, you're ready to take up its possible solutions. Don't rule out a solution if it doesn't appear logical at first glance. Even if it proves to be worthless later on, it can contain ideas of value for tomorrow's problems. The more possible solutions you consider, the better your final solution is apt to be.

C. *Evaluating the possible solutions.* When you're sure you've gathered up all the possible solutions, you're ready to compare them. Before you compare one with another, you should always weigh the advantages of one solution against its own disadvantages. *This is a definite time-saver for you.* If the disadvantages outweigh the advantages so much that the solution is impractical, *don't compare it with the other solutions.* The cure may be worse than the disease!

As a bit of special guidance, keep this thought in mind. Don't let your personal preferences or prejudices enter in when you're evaluating possible solutions to your problem—don't discard Smith's suggestion automatically just because he has bad breath or dandruff, or Jones's idea because you don't like his wife!

D. *Selecting the best solution.* A point well worth mentioning here, because it's so often overlooked, even by the experts, is that the solution you select could be a combination of two suggested solutions. For instance, you might take part of Black's idea, half of White's, and come up with a *gray solution* that fills the bill for you precisely.

So use your imagination! Once you've got your thinking in the groove on this, don't be afraid to swing out of the pattern once in a while. It's not that cut-and-dried!

3. TAKE THE APPROPRIATE ACTION.

In this step, you simply put the solution you've chosen, the decision you've made, into immediate effect. Use the techniques that fit your own personality and your way of doing things. But don't hesitate and waver now. The hard work is over. Take the appropriate action; issue the necessary instructions, and then—*Supervise the execution of your order.*

Although *supervision* is not considered as an integral part of the problem-solving process, your corrective action is only as good as your follow-up and your supervision. Don't be content with merely initiating the corrective action. Success will often depend on your ability and your willingness to supervise and check the results of your efforts.

Use your initiative,
your imagination, and your ingenuity

To discuss this technique, I'd like to tell you about the highly imaginative and ingenious methods the James F. Lincoln Electric

Company in Cleveland, Ohio, uses to get top production in their plant.

Incidentally, Andy Stone, their vice-president in charge of production and manufacturing tells me that their sales manager uses the same system to spur their salesmen to greater efforts, so it doesn't really matter whether you're engaged in industrial management, wholesaling, or retailing, you can use their system to your own benefit, too.

In fact, Dr. Harvey Bruce, District Superintendent for the Methodist Church in St. Louis, Missouri, tells me they use most of these same points to increase church membership and attendance. They just apply them in a slightly different approach, that's all. He says that they've been so successful they've set new attendance records in St. Louis for Methodist churches all over the world.

Dr. Bruce says this about his own methods: "I never ask anyone *if* he'll do something for me. I always let the other person know *I believe that he can do it,* that I have full confidence in his ability, and that I definitely trust him to do a good job. Then I go away and leave him alone. If you constantly look over a man's shoulder, you're intimating that you don't quite trust him to do a decent job for you. I assume that he will do a good job for me, and I'm seldom disappointed."

Now let me tell you about Lincoln Electric and you can see how close their methods are to those of Dr. Bruce. Lincoln Electric, by the way, is one of the pioneers in the field of profit sharing and production incentive systems that will motivate their employees to work harder and produce more. But first, let me tell you about some of their astonishing results before I tell you *their* plan of action.

1. The company's volume of business jumped from 5 million a year to 33 million a year, an increase of nearly 700 percent in nine years.
2. The cost of the manufactured article—arc-welding equipment—was cut in half in spite of a continued rise in the cost of raw materials.
3. The amount of dividends paid to stockholders increased fourfold—400 percent—in those nine years.

4. The annual average wage for every one of Lincoln's one thousand employees jumped 540 percent during that time.

Andy Stone's plan of action   How was all this possible? Here's Andy Stone himself to tell you:

"We used five basic steps in our production incentive and profit-sharing plan," says Andy. "You already know the results, so without wasting time, I'll tell you what those steps were; or I should say *are*— for we still use them, of course!

"1. *We set up production standards and then we encourage our employees to beat our system.*

"This is a challenge to every man and no one likes to turn down a dare. Our employees will use their imagination and ingenuity to beat the system, produce more, and thus earn more incentive pay. The more money they make for themselves, the more money they make for the company. This system inspires them to work harder—to want to produce more—to want to figure out better and more efficient ways of doing things.

"2. *We offer our employees complete security.*

"Once we got our system rolling, we never had to fire a single man. During our trial period we lost only two employees who were removed by the men themselves. If a man slows down the work of his fellow employee, they get rid of him for us. We take no action at all.

"Actually, the only time we've ever had to do anything, we had to step in to keep a man from being discharged. And that was only a matter of moving him to a job he was capable of doing! He wasn't maliciously trying to slow down production; he was doing the best job he knew how to do. It was up to us to match the man and the job. Under this system we can do that, and our employees back us up.

"3. *We let our employees set their own production goals.*

"Our men realize that management's ability to pay them depends upon their production of a quality item in quantity. No man needs to be told to work harder when he can make more money by doing so.

"4. *We let each man work in his own style.*

"We find that no matter how routine a man's job is, each employee will find some way of expressing his own individuality in his work. When we let them do that, they no longer worry about a supervisor popping up unexpectedly.

"If a man can do a better job standing up—he stands up. If he can do a better job sitting down—he sits down. Only three points enter the picture here: *Safety—quality—quantity*. Instead of hatching up trouble as they used to do, our people now use their brains to figure out what ability, what talent, and what ingenuity they can give to the company. And they come up with some amazing ideas of how to improve things and speed up production that would do justice to an inventive genius.

"5. *Last, we let our employees tell us how and where they need to improve.*

"Really, I don't think we ever punish or reprimand a man anymore. If we had to, he wouldn't stay with us. They've made management so easy for me, I almost worry about my own job security!"

Let me ask you this now. Do you consider this gaining power with people? Well, I'll guarantee you that a lot of other people do. Lincoln Electric's methods of gaining power with people have been so successful that during the last several years nearly a thousand top level business executives, personnel directors, and industrial psychologists have traveled to Cleveland to study them.

Look at it this way. You really have power with people *when they WANT to do what you want them to do*. That's the exact position Lincoln Electric holds in relation to their employees. Their employees want to do what Lincoln Electric wants them to do, and as a result, everyone makes more money.

I'd like also to point out that they do all this by fulfilling a man's basic subconscious needs and desires that we discussed a short time ago. In fact, they fill seven out of a man's nine subconscious needs in their program, and that's a terrific batting average. When you can do that, you know you'll gain power with people. The seven desires they take care of are: 1. *Emotional security,* 2. *Recognition of efforts,* 3. *Creative outlets,* 4. *A sense of personal power,* 5. *A feeling of belonging,* 6. *Ego-gratification,* and 7. *New experiences.*

Determine where you are now . . .

Determine where you now are in relation to your goals and measure your progress on a regular basis. If you worked for the J. C. Penney Company, you could measure your distance from the top management spot and know that your chances were good of making it, for the J. C. Penney people never bring in managers and executives from the outside. It's a standard policy at Penney's that all must start at the bottom. Every top Penney executive has done so.

I asked the chairman of the board who would take his place when he retires. His answer was simply this: "We'd hire a new office clerk!"

Sears, Roebuck follows the same policy. They never hire their store managers *off-the-street.* They work their way up through the system. When one top man retires at Sears, no less than fourteen others are promoted up the line.

Your biggest stumbling blocks here could be *premature satisfaction* and *loss of purpose and direction.* My files are full of cases like this. Here are only three examples to show you what I mean:

> An ambitious young automobile salesman, Harry T., reaches his goal of sales manager, and promptly runs out of steam. A year later, he's looking for a job.
>
> George D., a capable, fast-rising sales manager is put in charge of the entire midwest—and begins to slide, right on down the hill and out of the company.
>
> After a brilliant climb up the executive ladder, Howard L., a divisional manager, is named vice-president in charge of marketing—but his fire's burned out. In less than two years, he's starting all over again with a different firm.

What went wrong in these cases? Two things. One—*they mistook the beginning of achievement for the end.* The first mistake led to the second—*loss of purpose and direction.*

You can avoid failures like these if you learn to pace yourself. One of the best ways to do that is to———

Set realistic target dates . . .

Set realistic and reasonable target dates for reaching each one of your goals. Sometimes, a person hesitates to give himself a specific deadline for fear he might not reach it! If he misses, then he quits! But you'll never get anywhere if you're afraid to get on the road and start your trip. The simple solution is to revise your deadlines when you miss, or better yet—set a realistic and reasonable target date in the beginning. As the old saying goes, "Don't try to be a saint by Thursday." Take Jack Farmer, for instance—

"When I was in the army, I looked forward anxiously to the day of my return to civilian life," says Jack. "I wanted to go into business for myself, and I saved every cent I could so I could open my own men's clothing store.

"I gave myself a goal of five years to have the business completely paid for. At the end of the first year, business was good. The second year, things looked even better. And the third year went along well. I was only two years away from paying off the bank completely and realizing my goal.

"Then things began to go against me. A tough, hard-hitting competitor moved in across the street from me. My business began to drop off and I suddenly found I had to start cutting corners to make my bank payments.

"I panicked and instead of expanding my lines to meet my competition, I cut down even further in my store stock. Soon many of my shelves were empty.

"One day the vice president of my bank dropped in to buy some shirts. He looked at my empty shelves and the empty store, and asked why. We talked for a while and I told him my problem.

" 'You've given yourself an unrealistic deadline and in a sense— the wrong goal,' he said. 'You want to run a successful and prosperous clothing business. That's your real goal—not just paying off a bank in an unreasonably short time. You need to expand to meet your competition—not contract!'

"It was just that simple. I refinanced my loan, built up my stock and filled my empty shelves. Then I gave myself some reasonable and realistic target dates to pay off my business loan. That gave me new confidence and a brand new outlook on things. It's going great now."

Picture the rewards in your mind . . .

Picture in your mind the rewards that will be yours when you reach your goals. Some years back when Liberace was an unknown piano player playing in small smoke-filled nightclubs and out-of-the-way supper clubs, he came across two books that changed his life completely, *The Magic of Believing* * and *TNT: The Power Within You*.** These two books stress the importance of seeing in your mind's eye what you want to achieve in life. They both say that you should use your imagination to create the picture of what you want to do, to have, or to be, just as though you had already achieved it!

To do this, Liberace hit upon a most amazing and unusual idea. He had been dreaming of the day when he could play for a packed house in the famous Hollywood Bowl. *How can I speed the day when my dream will become a reality?* he thought. And then the flash of insight and inspiration came. *I'll rent a piano, have it transported to the Hollywood Bowl, and I'll put on a show, just as if the giant amphitheater were filled with my cheering fans!*

Liberace set about at once to make the necessary arrangements. He did so quietly, telling no one, for he knew people would think that he'd lost his mind completely. When he came on stage and made his opening bow, he visualized every seat in that vast and empty bowl with someone sitting in it. He could hear in his imagination the thun-

---

* Claude M. Bristol, *The Magic of Believing* (Englewood Cliffs, N.J., Prentice-Hall, Inc., 1957).

** Claude M. Bristol and Harold Sherman, *TNT: The Power Within You*, revised 1966, and retitled *The New TNT—Miraculous Power Within You* (Englewood Cliffs, N.J., Prentice-Hall, Inc.).

derous applause as he began his concert. Throughout his entire two-hour program, he continued to play and sing and keep up a running patter to his imaginary audience. He was dressed in his best sparkling costume—pretending to the full that the great Liberace had really arrived. As he finished his final number he saw his audience rise to give him a standing ovation. He responded with encore after encore, bowing time and again in his appreciation. And then it was over and the Bowl became empty and deserted once again.

But four years later, this exact scene was repeated. *But this time —it was real; this time every seat was filled with real live people!* Success and acclaim had come to Liberace. His dreams of playing to a full house in the vast Hollywood Bowl, which he had rehearsed to himself with such feeling and with such deep faith, had become a reality!

If you can picture in your own mind your goals, with perhaps just a tiny bit of the faith and the imagination Liberace had, you'll succeed in reaching them, too.

POINTS TO REMEMBER

To succeed in life, you need three big factors:

1. A GOAL.
2. A PLAN to reach that goal.
3. PEOPLE to help you put your plan into effect so you can reach your goal.

Benefits you'll gain

Some of the benefits you'll gain when you plan your campaign for power with people are:

1. Planning your campaign for power with people will give you both purpose and direction.
2. Establishing your goals will help you decide what you want to do and what you want to be.

3. Planning your campaign for power with people will give you perseverance and determination to succeed.

Steps in the problem-solving process

1. Recognize the problem.
2. Make an estimate of the situation by . . .
   a. *Determining the exact cause.*
   b. *Determining all possible solutions.*
   c. *Evaluating the possible solutions.*
   d. *Selecting the best solution.*
3. Take the appropriate action.

A plan of action

Follow this skeleton plan and tailor it to fit your own needs:

1. Establish your short-range and your long-range goals.
2. Set up your tangible and your intangible goals.
3. Learn to recognize obstacles, road-blocks, and problems. Get rid of them, go around them, or solve them.
4. Use your initiative, your imagination, and your ingenuity.
5. Determine where you now are in relation to your goals and measure your progress on a regular basis.
6. Set realistic and reasonable dates for reaching each one of your goals.
7. Picture in your mind the rewards that will be yours when you reach your goals.

4

How to Use Simple Instructions— Yet Get Amazing Results!

Time and again you've no doubt been told that if you want to accomplish great things in business and industry— if you want to be of service to your community—if you want to succeed in a professional field—you must know how to work through others. You must be able to control and influence other people. And you can do this if you give clear, concise, and positive orders that are easy to understand. Then you must follow up to make sure your instructions are promptly and properly carried out.

You say you don't have a job where you tell others what to do? You never give instructions or orders to anyone at all? Funny thing. Might be just a coincidence, but you sound exactly like some people who tried to tell me the same story last week.

For instance, Helen Andrews told me she was only a housewife. "I never give orders to anyone. I don't have a job," she said. Five minutes after she told me that, she was speaking to more than a hundred volunteer workers to tell them what their duties were going to be in the annual Red Cross fund drive. Helen's job? Oh, she'd been placed in charge of organizing and directing the collection for the entire southeast part of her city. Her area alone has a population of more than twenty thousand. But she's only a housewife, or so she says!

Then there was Annie, the pert little blonde nurse in St. John's pediatric ward. "My job isn't to give orders; it's to see that the doctor's orders are carried out," she said. "Oh, excuse me a minute. I want to say something to that new orderly. He never seems to get anything right.

"Jack, I told you to take those specimens down to the lab—not to the X-ray clinic! And where are the pictures of the Smith boy's leg? Doctor's still waiting to see them. And what about the iodine and roller bandages I told you to bring up from supply this morning? I wish you'd learn to listen to my instructions once in a while!"

Change your mind yet? All right then. Now that you do agree that sometimes you, too, must give instructions to other people, let's see what advantages will be yours when you make sure the job is understood, supervised, and accomplished. Remember that when you keep your orders simple, concise, and easy to understand, you'll get some really amazing results.

BENEFITS YOU'LL GAIN

You can motivate people—

You can motivate people to do their best for you when they know exactly what their jobs are and when they know exactly what you want them to do. People will do a better job for you when you tell them what their duties are, exactly what you want done, and precisely what results you expect from them. Many times a person fails to do a decent job for you only because he doesn't understand specifically what you want. It's up to you to tell him what you expect and when and where you expect it. Do this, and you'll get results.

People will respond—

People will respond quickly to orders that are concise, clear, positive, and easy to understand. You'll get much better and faster results from people when your instructions are simple, concise, and to the point. On the other hand, you can easily create confusion and chaos if you overstate your order by adding too many details. Tell people in simple terms what you want done, but don't tell them how to do it—that is, if you want the best and fastest results.

You can emphasize results—

When you keep your instructions simple and to the point, you can emphasize results—not methods. You can motivate people to do their best for you when you emphasize skill, not rules; results, not methods. To do this, *use mission-type orders.* (A mission-type order tells a person what you want done and when you want it, but it doesn't tell him how to do it. The "how-to" is left up to him.) A mission-type order opens the door wide so people can use their imagination, initiative, and ingenuity to do the job for you. No matter what your line is, this can lead to a better way of doing things. If you're in business, improved methods will mean increased profits for you.

You can decentralize and supervise—

When people know exactly what you want and precisely what their jobs are, you can decentralize responsibility and supervise their work more effectively. If you're in business or industry, sales, or even in the military, decentralization of your work and better supervision of your people are two concrete benefits you can enjoy when you make sure people know exactly what their jobs are. People like to know that you're available for advice and counsel if you're needed. However, they'll always resent oversupervision or harassment. When you emphasize results, not methods, you'll cut your supervisory requirements to the bone.

Proper supervision will *help* a person do his job. Improper supervision *forces* him to do it. The real test of a foreman or a supervisor, a lieutenant or a sergeant, a social chairman or the director of a Red Cross fund drive, is not how good that individual is at bossing and issuing orders, but rather, how little supervising has to be done because of the organization of the work, the decentralization of responsibility, and the simplicity of his instructions.

Simple plans and simple orders are two of the cornerstones of success

The University of Arkansas has turned out winning football teams for many a year now. Yet their coach tells me the Razorbacks use no more than a dozen simple plays. But every single player knows exactly what everyone else is going to do on each one of those plays. "A simple play, executed with drill-like precision and speed, is more likely to move the ball and gain the needed yardage than a detailed and complicated one," he says.

The army uses the same principle. Simplicity is a maxim of war. The best plan will be one that avoids complexities in design, presentation, and execution. Such a plan is better understood by everyone. A simple plan reduces the chance for error, and its simplicity speeds up its execution.

In business, the most profitable companies are those who have simple strategic concepts; clear plans and programs of execution; specific assignment of decision-making responsibilities; simplified accounting and administrative procedures; fast, direct communications. In short, all aspects of the business will be kept as simple as possible at all times.

Now that you know some of the benefits of issuing simple orders and instructions, let's take a look at some of the *techniques you can use to create simple instructions.*

**TECHNIQUES YOU CAN USE
TO GAIN THOSE BENEFITS**

1. *First,* make sure the need for an order exists.
2. *Next,* be sure you know the result you want.
3. *Then,* and not till then—issue clear, concise, and positive orders that are easy to understand.
4. Disguise your orders as suggestions or requests.
5. Check for understanding.
6. Check for progress.
7. Offer to help when and where you can.

And now in detail. . . .

Make sure the need for an order exists

If you're in charge, people already know it   You don't have to issue an order just to prove you're the boss. If you're in charge, people are usually well aware of that fact already. You don't have to prove it by issuing some unnecessary order.

When a foreman or a supervisor is new on the job, or if he's afraid he's about to get the axe, you'll see this happen. And once in a while, an executive will go "power mad" and start punching buttons just to see people jump. In the army, young second lieutenants and newly promoted corporals are prone to make this mistake. However, the services are not unique in this. I've seen this first basic rule violated again and again in business establishments and industrial plants.

"That's an order, damn it!" the young foreman yelled. "Don't talk back to me. They're still on the time clock so get 'em back on their feet. And that's an order!"

I stood with that young foreman, Barton F., watching the change of shifts in his department—stock preparation. It was just short of 7:00—the official plant time for punching out on the clock.

Why was I there? Well, I'd been called in as a management consultant by this particular rubber company. They were in deep trouble because of their extremely low employee morale. Continual acts of vandalism—even sabotage—had wrecked some expensive major items of equipment and had slowed production to the point the company was losing valuable customers because they couldn't fill their orders on time. The pressure was on, from the chairman of the board down through the plant manager to the last supervisor, to get things straightened out. That's why I was there: to help them find their problem and solve it.

The day shift had already reported; they stood at their machines waiting to be told about the day's production. They needed only their supervisor's OK to start rolling. The graveyard shift was tired; it was the end of their working day. They'd been hard at it since eleven o'clock the night before. Now that they were finished, they were squatting down on their haunches to rest, leaning against the iron railings around the heavy machinery, or sitting on stacks of rubber skids just waiting for the seven o'clock whistle to blow.

The young foreman called his outgoing shift supervisor over. "Get those men on their feet!" he snapped. "You know I don't allow anyone to sit down while he's working in my department. I'm not running a damned rest home!"

"But Bart, my men are all through work," the night supervisor protested. "You know we have a ten minute changeover period. They're tired and they're simply waiting for the whistle to blow so they can leave and go home. They're not working now."

"Don't talk back to me!" the foreman yelled. "I'm still the boss in this department. They're still on the clock, so get 'em on their feet. And that's an order, damn it!"

Here's how you can make sure the need for an order exists   An order is needed in only four specific situations:

1. To start some action.
2. To correct a mistake in the action or to solve a problem.

3. To speed up the action or to slow it down.
4. To stop the action.

Now I'll bet you're sitting there right now trying to think up more times when you might need an order. For example, you might be thinking, "What if I have to change direction?" Do me a favor, will you please? Just slip that question under number 2—to correct a mistake in the action or to solve a problem. Don't fight it—let it!

It's more important to remember that you must know how to make an estimate of the situation before you can issue any order or before you can change or modify it. But we don't have the time to go over that one again; we've already covered it. If you've forgotten how to make an estimate of the situation, just turn back to Chapter 3 and refresh your memory if you'd like.

Be sure you know the result you want

Keep in mind—you should emphasize *results, not methods*. You must know what you want before you can tell anyone to do anything. That's why it's so important that you keep your attention focused on the end result, not the techniques used to get there. You see, it isn't at all necessary that you know *how* the job is to be done; that's up to the person doing the job to figure out for himself.

One of the best ways to determine the result you want is to use the principle of *backward planning*. You can use this method for anything from trimming your Christmas tree to decorating the church dining room for a fund-raising supper, planning an elaborate and complicated wedding or a pleasure trip down through Old Mexico. If it's a tree or a room you're decorating, remember *that which you see first goes on last* and you'll never go wrong. Keep that in mind and you won't sit there glaring at your Yuletide tree wondering how you can get the lights put on over the angel hair and tinsel without tearing everything apart. Or you won't find that in your haste and enthusiasm to decorate the church dining room for the benefit supper, you've hidden the main speaker's table from view by a wall of festive crepe streamers.

Or take such a complicated thing as a formal wedding. You can simplify it by getting down on paper the end results you want to see on the wedding day. If you want to go all out on this, call that "D Day" if you like. Then start plotting a backward course from there and number your days like this: D minus 30; D minus 29; D minus 28, etc. On each day show what the end results must be and indicate what has to be done and by whom to get those results.

Plan the big event like that, just one day at a time, and you'll find the problems and the complications will melt away for you when you use *backward planning*. (And I speak with the voice of personal experience. I know it will work; I've already given away one daughter in marriage.)

Take a simple thing like planning a trip. I've seen people end up with frazzled nerves, a pile of broken pencils, and chewed up fingernails trying to figure out what day they had to leave Kansas City so they could be in Los Angeles by Friday and see Pike's Peak, the Grand Canyon, and the Painted Desert on the way. But there's no need for that.

Backward planning for a trip is simple once you get the hang of it. Just put yourself in Los Angeles on Friday and work backward until you reach Kansas City. You can pin-point your departure time almost to the hour and minute you need to put the last piece of luggage in the trunk.

Once you're sure of the result you want, just tell the other person what it is. That should be no problem at all if you'll remember to——

Issue positive orders
that are easy to understand

Your order can be oral or written. Your choice will depend upon what's to be done and how complex the task is. If a lot of people are doing the work and there are a lot of deadlines to meet, the least you'll need is a notebook to keep track of who's doing what and when.

To issue clear, concise, and positive orders that are easy to understand, follow these guidelines:

1. Fit your order to the job to be done.
2. Use simple words and simple terms.
3. Concentrate on a single point.
4. If it's a written order—
   a. Use your own language.
   b. Develop your own style.
   c. Don't worry too much about grammar.

Fit your order to the job to be done   You don't need a five paragraph field order to say "Forward March!" But if you're working in a lab with chemicals, a carefully written, step-by-step plan is a must. But don't confuse all your previous detailed planning with the final order that's to be given. An extremely complex operation can be put in gear with a simple order. For instance, General Dwight Eisenhower kicked off the Normandy invasion in World War II with a simple 23 word sentence:

"You will enter the continent of Europe and undertake operations aimed at the heart of Germany and the destruction of her armed forces."

That was the order that launched more than four million men, five thousand naval vessels, five thousand fighter planes, and six thousand bombers into the battle for Europe. Of course, months of planning preceded the actual invasion. Hundreds of staff officers drew up the detailed plans for operation *Overland*. But in the end, all these forces, millions of men and thousands of ships, planes, and tanks were set in motion with that *single simple 23 word sentence!*

Use simple words and simple terms   I have actually seen people go out of their way to use big words to drive another person to a dictionary. Perhaps they wanted to appear wise and well-educated. If that was their objective, they defeated their purpose. I once knew an army officer who loved to use such words as *obfuscate,* for instance. If confusion was his goal, he succeeded, for the word *obfuscate* means to *cloud, confuse, darken,* or *muddle.*

Instead of using such simple verbs like *make* or *do*, Captain J. L. used *construct, fabricate, accomplish, perform, consummate,* or *effect.* He never *started* anything; instead, he *initiated, commenced,* or *inaugurated* everything. He never *sent* a message; he always *forwarded, transmitted,* or *communicated* it. Nor did he *send out* information; he *circulated* it or *promulgated* it or *disseminated* it. Nor did he use little words such as *if, so, for,* and *but.* He always made certain to replace them with *in the event that, therefore, on behalf of, nevertheless.* Captain J. L. might on occasion admit that some of the "governmental federalese" needed *improvement,* but he always wanted you to say *amelioration!*

Now it could well be that people like Captain J. L. caused Mr. Joseph A. Ecclesine to write this article for *Printers' Ink* Magazine.*

Big Words Are for the Birds

When you come right down to it, there is no law that says you have to use big words when you write or talk.

There are lots of small words, and good ones, that can be made to say all the things you want to say, quite as well as the big ones. It may take a bit more time to find them at first. But it can be well worth it, for all of us know what they mean. Some small words, more than you might think, are rich with just the right feel, the right taste, as if made to help you say a thing the way it should be said.

Small words can be crisp, brief, terse—go to the point, like a knife. They have a charm all their own. They dance, twist, turn, sing. Like sparks in the night they light the way for the eyes of those who read. They are the grace notes of prose. You know what they say the way you know a day is bright and fair—at first sight. And you find, as you read, that you like the way they say it. Small words are gay. And they can catch large thoughts and hold them for all to see, like rare stones in rings of gold, or joy in the eyes of a child. Some make you feel, as well as see: the cold deep dark of night, the hot salt sting of tears.

---

* Joseph A. Ecclesine, "Big Words Are for the Birds," *Printers' Ink,* 1961.

Small words move with ease where big words stand still—or, worse, bog down and get in the way of what you want to say. There is not much, in all truth, that small words will not say— and say quite well.

Let me wrap up this idea of using simple words and simple terms by pointing out that it's the simple things that last longest and wear best. The simplest writing is always the best writing because it's the easiest to understand.

Nearly two thousand years ago a man who walked by the Sea of Galilee understood the principle of simplicity well. Everything in His life was simple: His clothing and His food; His stories and His parables. His language and His words. Yet His message is still studied today, for, even though complicated by man, the order He gave was clear, concise, positive, and easy to understand, for He simply said, *"Follow me."*

Concentrate on a single point—don't scatter your fire   Even though there might be a multitude of details to be taken care of, you can handle them if you'll just keep your eye fixed on your final objective. It's easy to get things done with people and to achieve power with them if you don't complicate things and make it difficult for yourself.

Don't clutter up your mind with trivia that confuses and clouds the main job to be done. Just keep it simple. Stick to the basic fundamentals—the essential facts.

"Keep the fundamentals before you," says Charles B. Roth in his book, *How to Make $25,000 a Year Selling.**

"The fundamentals of salesmanship, which are often ignored by unsuccessful salesmen, are not intricate or difficult," Mr. Roth says. "They are basic and simple—such things as knowing how to win and hold attention, how to establish confidence, how to get the sale set up for the close, and how to close it.

---

* Charles B. Roth, *How to Make $25,000 a Year Selling* (Englewood Cliffs, N.J., Prentice-Hall, Inc.).

"One of the fundamentals," he concludes, "is to *concentrate on a single point and not scatter your fire.*"

When your order is written, use these pointers

USE YOUR OWN LANGUAGE. Don't freeze up when you ɟick up a pen. Use the same kind of language you'd use to tell your neighbor about the fish you caught last weekend down on the lake. Add whatever technical terms you need, make the rest simple one- and two-syllable words, and you'll get your message across without any trouble at all.

DEVELOP YOUR OWN STYLE. Don't try to impress someone by writing a letter or an order the way you *think* they want it written. There's no such thing as a standard letter to follow as an infallible guide. That's why government writers are always in hot water. They copy someone else's style to the letter, mistakes and all! Develop your own distinctive style. Let your letters reflect your personality so vividly everyone will know who wrote it even when you forget to sign it.

DON'T WORRY TOO MUCH ABOUT GRAMMAR. The way a word is used is more important than the way a book of grammar says it should be used. The rules of grammar reflect only the usage of yesterday. Besides, you don't really have to be a grammarian to recognize a good sentence. After all, the first requirement of grammar is that you focus your reader's attention on the meaning you want to convey. If you take care to make your meaning clear, your grammar will usually take care of itself.

Disguise your orders as suggestions or requests

If people have any initiative, you'll get far better results from suggestions rather than direct orders. People simply won't react to direct commands unless they're in the army. "And even that's no guarantee," Colonel Fairfield says.

"I spent more than 25 years in service, and I doubt if I gave more than a dozen direct orders in that length of time," Colonel Bob goes on to say. "And most of those commands were given to my jeep driver, like 'Stop here; turn left; turn right.'

"Seriously though, I always got good results by asking a man to do something or by suggesting that he try it a certain way. You know there's no law that says a colonel can't say 'Why don't you try it this way? What is your opinion, Sergeant? Would you be good enough to . . . I wish you would . . . I desire.'

"I'll tell you this much. Disguising your orders as suggestions or requests works far better than yelling at a man to 'Do this!' or 'Do that!' When you yell at a man, you're just inviting him to yell back at you!"

A good way to put this guideline into action is to use it on your children and your husband or your wife. Experiment a little. Pick up some experience around the house and soon you'll be ready to go out and play the game like a regular old pro!

Check for understanding by—

1. Having people repeat oral orders back to you.
2. Asking people questions to see if they understand.
3. Having them ask you questions when they don't understand.

Have oral orders repeated back to you   I can think of no exception whatever to this rule. The first time you break it, sure as green apples, things'll go wrong. And if people misinterpret your order or your instructions, it's a cinch you'll not get the results you want. You can't possibly get the job done that way.

So make this a hard and fast rule to follow. Paste it in your hat. Oh, I know that once in a while a person will get irritated when you ask him to repeat your orders. He thinks you're insulting his intelligence. Well, my friend, so be it. He'll just have to feel that way. Don't worry; he'll soon get over it. However, if he's extremely sensitive about it, you can move right into step number 2 by——

Asking him questions to see if he understands your order   For instance, you could say, "How do you plan on tackling this problem, John? What are your ideas on how to handle this, Sam?"

Or you could use an approach like one of these:

> "Do you understand why this small plate goes on first?"
>
> "Do you see now why this part has to go on last?"
>
> "Do you know why the temperature must be kept at a constant 68 degrees?"

Or you can use the third way to check for progress which is to——

Have them ask you questions when they don't understand Normally, if a person doesn't understand what you want, he'll ask you to clarify it for him. You can give this procedure a boost by asking, "Are there any questions?"

If you're giving instructions to a group, don't assume everything's understood just because no one asks a question. Many times, a person will have a question, or there'll be a point he doesn't understand, but he doesn't want to expose his ignorance in front of the group. For instance——

Remember your high school days. The teacher asks, "Are there any questions?" Not a hand goes up anywhere. "Class is dismissed, then," the teacher says, and immediately half a dozen students who were afraid they'd appear stupid in front of the others flock around the desk to have some point explained.

Of course, if that teacher happens to have measurements of 36-24-36, my premise on this point could be entirely defeated!

Check for progress

1. Inspection and supervision.
2. Having the person check back when the job is done.
3. Holding a formal critique and review.

Inspection and supervision   Supervise people's progress by inspecting their work. *A person does well only if the boss inspects.* To inspect and check a person's work without appearing to snoop, be nosy, and harass is an art. But simply asking a person how he's getting along is not inspecting. To inspect and supervise thoroughly, use this checklist:

1. *Allocate a definite amount of time each day for your inspections.* Check some phase of your work every day. Never let a day go by without inspecting something. Monday mornings and Friday afternoons are the most critical periods of the working week.

2. *Select your inspection points before you inspect.* Before you inspect, pick your points of interest and the potential trouble spots for your inspection. Review these points before you inspect; know what you're doing. Never inspect less than three nor more than eight specific points during any one inspection period.

3. *When you inspect, check only these points.* Don't let people lead you astray. This can become a cat and mouse game if you allow it to. Stick to the inspection points you've selected; don't look at the points they'd like you to inspect. Any time a person wants to show off how well something is done, you know something else hasn't been done. If you're looking at the oil, water, and battery on Monday, don't let 'em show you the tires, gas, and horn 'til Tuesday.

4. *When you inspect, bypass your chain of command.* This is a must. No other kind of inspection is worth the effort. Always check the person who's actually doing the work. Don't ask his foreman or his supervisor. I can tell you their answers before you leave your office.

5. *When you inspect, listen—don't talk.* Remember the purpose of your inspection. It's to gather information and check progress, not to let people know how wise and important you are. Since you're the boss, they know that already.

6. *Vary your routine.* Don't inspect the same points every Monday, the same ones on Tuesday, etc. Change things around. Keep people on their toes all the time.

Have the person check back when the job is finished   If the task is quite complicated, set up intermediate checkpoints. For instance, if you're writing a book, chances are the editor will want to approve only two or three chapters at a time—not the whole book at once. It's the best way to keep a person on the right track before he goes off on a tangent and ruins the whole project.

Hold a formal critique and review   The military services always do this when they run field problems. Every exercise is followed up by a thorough discussion of what was right and what was wrong. You don't have to be as stiff and formal about it as they are, perhaps, but it's a good way of getting the bugs worked out so you can get off to a fresh start and run a clean show the next time.

Offer to help when and where you can

"Everyone appreciates it, especially when the going gets tough, if the boss stops and offers to help," says Jim Henderson, president of the Henderson General Contracting Company in St. Louis. "Getting your hands dirty once in a while is a good way to boost morale and it won't cost you more than half a buck or so to get your boots cleaned and your shirt washed. However, before you pitch in to help, you ought to remember that *when the boss gets involved too deep in the work, he's no longer the boss.* You must know where to draw the line."

POINTS TO REMEMBER

Benefits you'll gain

1. You can motivate people to do their best for you when they know exactly what their jobs are and when they know exactly what you want them to do.
2. People will respond quickly to orders that are concise, clear, positive, and easy to understand.
3. When you keep your instructions simple and to the point, you can emphasize results—not methods.
4. When people know exactly what you want and precisely

what their jobs are, you can decentralize responsibility and supervise more effectively.

5. Simple plans and simple orders are two of the cornerstones of success.

Techniques you can use
to gain these benefits

1. First—make sure the need for an order exists.
2. Next, be sure you know the result you want.
3. Then issue clear, concise, and positive orders that are easy to understand.
4. Disguise your orders as suggestions or requests.
5. Check for understanding.
6. Check for progress.
7. Offer to help when and where you can.

5

How to Be Your Own Self-Starter

A lot of good plans can go down the drain if you're not ready when the right time comes. Pearl Harbor will live forever in our country's memory as the classic historical example of a nation's failure to be ready. All sorts of defense plans had to be scrapped after the Japanese attack was over. Too many of our battleships lay ruined at the bottom of the bay.

But you don't have to be in the military to benefit from using the principle of readiness. It can be used in business and industry and most other fields as well. If you're a teacher, you'll be able to give better instruction with a good lesson plan than if you're completely unprepared.

Or if you're a preacher, you might get some inspiration from the Higher Power when you're in your pulpit on Sunday morning. You might also get struck by lightning. Some advance work on your sermon will make you feel a lot more at ease behind your lectern.

If you're a student, you know how uncomfortable and embarrassed you can feel when you're called on and you're not prepared. No examination is ever hard if you're ready for it and if you know all the answers. Or maybe it would work out better if you knew all the questions!

BENEFITS YOU'LL GAIN

Now that you've got these general ideas in mind, let me give you three specific benefits you'll gain by proper preparation in your drive to succeed and gain power with people.

1. You'll never be caught off guard by your competitors or your enemies.
2. You'll build a reputation for getting things done.
3. You'll not miss the opportunity for promotion and advancement.

You'll never be caught off guard by your enemies when you're prepared

During World War II, the 71st Infantry Regiment required every man to be dressed, fully armed, and manning his battle station at first light. Communications were checked from the squad leader up to the regimental commander. Readiness reports were made through command channels from the bottom to the top. After daylight—and only if the regimental commander decided that an enemy attack was not imminent—the troops were allowed to eat breakfast and get on with the day's routine activities of fighting a war.

This early morning *stand-to,* as it was called, was never popular, even in combat. Company commanders made one request after another to get this stringent requirement relaxed, especially for men who'd been on guard or night duty. But their requests were never granted by our regimental commander, Colonel Porter, and I, like everyone else, beefed about this *unreasonable order*—until the morning of January 1, 1945.

That morning, near Rimling, France, the 2nd Battalion of the 71st, commanded by Lieutenant Colonel Edgar S. McKee, was attacked by the 17th and 37th Panzer Grenadier Regiments. The initial assault of five companies against Company F was beaten back with heavy losses to the Germans.

After this engagement (which lasted for 2 full days and 3 more German regiments) was over, the 2nd Battalion was awarded the Presidential Unit Citation. The Battalion was credited with blunting the German High Command's attempt to drive a wedge between the Third and Seventh U. S. Armies so they could push on through southern France to the Mediterranean.

Never again did I—or anyone else—say another word about the *unreasonable* morning stand-to. Not a single man died in his sleeping bag that morning. Being ready had saved our lives.

Now you may not have to fight off your enemies at first light, but being prepared and ready for anything can be a valuable weapon to use in the in-fighting of today's executive jungle. Or if you're in politics, being prepared can get you elected and keep you in office.

If you're a lawyer, please tell me this: How many cases have you won without being ready—without proper preparation? It only happens on TV, doesn't it? Perry Mason always made it look so easy by some brilliant last minute maneuver. But since I'm not Perry Mason, I always make an effort to be ready; I recommend you do the same. *And the key to being prepared is to become your own self-starter.*

You'll build a reputation for getting things done

About the finest reputation you can build with your boss, or anyone else, is to have it said you know how to get things done. That makes you one of the *can-do* variety, a type that's almost extinct today. Such people are always sought after because they've become so rare.

"Military people are the most ingenious scroungers you'll ever meet," says Peter J. Ross, an expediter for Zenith Corporation's Springfield, Missouri, plant. Pete's job is to get raw materials and supplies shipped into Zenith's production line from their suppliers at a rate that's faster than humanly possible.

"My job as supply officer for the 3rd Battalion of the 19th Regiment helped prepare me for my job here at Zenith," Pete says. "How?

Because a GI has to make do with whatever's at hand. Like back in 1953, I built a 24 head shower unit for my battalion on Cheju-Do from *surplus* 55 gallon drums, *salvage* water faucets and shower heads, some *old* pipe, and *scrap* lumber, all *borrowed* from the island's engineer supply dump on a midnight requisition.

"The water for my shower had to be stolen from the gravity flow pipe that ran from the mountains to the Chinese prisoners' compound. I had to steal it for if everyone who wanted water had been allowed to tap the main line it would have exhausted the supply before it could reach the POWs.

"And if Chinese prisoners went dirty while their American captors kept clean, the International Red Cross would say 'Tsk, tsk,' and we just couldn't have that! So to tap the main line was a court-martial offense. But I never got caught for we piped the line at night and buried it underground all at the same time.

"I've seen two- and three-room 'houses' in Korea built from artillery ammo boxes. Washing machines can be assembled from a variety of machine parts and lots of imagination. Stoves for bunkers come from five-gallon lard cans while 81 mortar shell cases make excellent stove pipes.

"I've often heard it said the U. S. Army is held together by plywood, green tape, and carbon paper, and so help me—I believe it!"

Next time you complain to the boss you can't get the job done because you don't have the right materials or the proper tools, think about the shower unit Pete built from odds and ends. Maybe you'll get inspired and build your own reputation for getting things done.

You'll not miss the opportunity for promotion and advancement

A great many years ago when I suffered, but survived, the loss of my first childhood sweetheart, my dad gave me this bit of advice about the female sex:

"A woman is like a streetcar, son," he said. "If you miss the first one, don't worry about it. There'll be another one along in ten minutes!"

I wish I could say the same thing about opportunity, but I can't. At the same time, I don't want to beat the old drum of "opportunity knocks but once," but the way I look at it, there's no sense in missing your chance when it comes along because you're not prepared.

Army and Navy and Air Force officer personnel files bulge with names of those passed over for promotion simply because they failed to prepare themselves for high command. For every Eisenhower, Bradley, and Patton, there are thousands who miss their stars because they didn't aim for them.

I know that sometimes promotion and advancement come from being at the right place at the right time. I also know successful people somehow make a habit of being at that exact place at precisely the right time. Either that, or they create that time and place themselves. *They become their own self-starters.*

To sum it up, then, it's a matter of being ready so you'll not miss your chance. This thought leads me naturally to my next point: *How to become your own self-starter so you can be prepared to gain the benefits.*

Now in previous chapters I've given you certain specific techniques you can use to gain the benefits. In this chapter I'm going to do it just a bit differently. Since not being ready is usually the end result of plain old procrastination, I'm going to help you shake that bad habit of always and forever putting things off by giving you——

THIRTY-THREE SELF-STARTERS

Pin-point your goal   Don't waste time and energy just because you're not sure of what you want to do or where you want to go. Know what you're doing and where you're going. You'll get things done faster when you do. Ask yourself these questions: "What do I *really* want to do? Where do I *really* want to go?" Then give yourself a straight and honest answer. Level with yourself.

Make a list of everything that needs to be done   Make up a list just as you would a grocery shopping list. Then cross off each item as you do it. That way, you gain the satisfaction of having done part of the job. Your attention will automatically go to the next item down the line. You can use your own time basis for this; it depends on what you need. The important thing is: *Do it!*

Put what needs to be done right in front of you   When there's some distasteful task you don't want to do, it's easy to hide it away under something else. Your goal here should be *first things first*.

An old saying is: *Happiness lies, not in doing what you like to do, but, in liking what you have to do.* I used to spoof that idea when I was younger; the older I get, the more truth I find in it, though I still don't like it!

Concentrate on the essentials   I once knew a businessman who created nothing but chaos in his plant simply because he didn't know how to establish priorities in the work to be done. Every project to him was a crash. He sent out dozens of red-bordered memos marked "Urgent" to his department foremen and administrative staff every week.

But when everything is marked "Urgent," then "Urgent" becomes "Routine."

Efficiency experts like Raymond Bishop are paid fabulous fees to show people how to get things done. Listen to Ray's tip on this; it's yours for free!

"Problems can be solved by establishing priorities," Ray says. "Make up a list of the most urgent tasks facing you right now. *Give each job a different priority. No two jobs can have the same number.*

"Then dig right in on Priority Number One and stick with it until it's done. Then go for Priority Number Two and do it the same way. Don't worry if you finish only one or two jobs a day. The point is—you're making progress now where before you were stalemated. You're getting things done by taking care of your most urgent problems first.

"In short, use the approach of *first things first; one thing at a time.*

If you can't solve your problems this way, chances are you couldn't handle them in any other way. Once you get this system rolling, stick with it; you'll clear away the debris on a daily basis."

Keep reselling yourself on the benefits you'll gain No salesman worthy of the name would try to close a prospect once, and then quit. The normal reaction of everyone is to say "No" the first time around. Remind yourself of this when you're trying to motivate yourself to do a job that's not especially interesting. For instance, it'd be a lot more fun to settle back in the old easy chair with a beer and watch TV than to record some new information in Smith's dossier. But, drinking a beer and watching the tube'll not give you power with people, especially Smith.

If you want to stimulate yourself to do something that's tedious, but necessary, push yourself to get with it. Get it over. Remind yourself of the rewards for doing it. If there aren't any, then you're collecting the wrong information, or you're shooting at the wrong target.

Give yourself a small part of the job to do When a person has a big job to do, he hates to start. He puts it off until the last possible moment. Watch a small boy practicing the piano. He'll play the song he knows best over and over rather than start on the new one he doesn't know. If you have some big job to do, break it down into parts. If you must call a hundred people, break your list down into five smaller lists of twenty names each. Then you can do a fifth at a time and the job becomes easy. To write a 65,000 word book is a tough job. But to write a book with twelve to fifteen chapters makes it much easier to do!

People on the Alcoholics Anonymous program don't try to stay sober the rest of their lives. "Couldn't make it that way," they say "Too big a job. We do it the easy way; one day at a time!"

Develop a written step-by-step plan The results of putting it down in writing are so amazing it seems to work like magic. A vague and nebulous idea will change to a concrete and specific fact when it's down on paper. That is—if it's at all worthwhile.

The process of writing it down forces you to be specific. If you check your ideas later on, you can get even more specific. Writing it down will help you see clearly other plans you just couldn't visualize when you were carrying it around up there in your head.

Make up some alternate plans   The amateur is satisfied with himself when he comes up with the *one best way* to do something. But the professional knows you need a pocketful of techniques if the *best* method fails. He knows how to travel the back roads and detours when the freeway is blocked.

Make a decision   Don't be so afraid of making a mistake that you procrastinate and do nothing. Fear of failure and possible embarrassment causes most indecision. *But the successful man only has to be right 51 percent of the time!*

When you have enough facts together to make a decision, do so. Don't worry about the decision after you've made it. The time to "worry" about a situation is before you act—not afterward!

Emphasize doing—not doing perfectly   When you feel you must do everything just so, you often find you can't start a new job. As long as you don't do anything, you don't run the risk of failure. When you keep your good ideas to yourself, your boss can't tell you they're wrong. The writer with his stuff in the desk drawer need never fear a critic.

"To make an honest mistake is not the end of the world," says Reverend Maurice Clay. "It's when you continually repeat that same mistake, *knowing that it's wrong*—then you ought to get concerned."

Why do pencils have erasers? People make mistakes. The man who's never made a mistake has yet to do anything. Nothing can be predicted right down to the letter, especially when people are part of the act, so you must experiment. Watch the results you get.

Figure out your reasons for putting things off   If you find you can't get started on a certain project, ask yourself these questions:

1. Do I really think the results are worth the effort?
2. Do I honestly think I can do the job?

If you can't motivate yourself to do a certain job, it's either not worth the effort, or you're afraid you can't do it. Find out what's wrong. Then correct it.

Get your problems down on paper   If you can figure out problems in your head, you're better than I am. The average person can't even add a single column of a few figures in his head. He has to see it in black and white in front of him before he can get the right answer. Merely thinking about a problem is usually the worst way to solve it. Put your problem down on paper so you can limit it. Fence it in with verbal barbed wire to clarify your thinking. Define it in specific and exact down-to-earth terms.

When you're tackling any problem, always approach it with the time honored question-words *what, when, where, why, who.*

Use your energy for action—not for worrying   Worrying uses up large amounts of energy. Ask any experienced worrier; he'll tell you that for sure. If you want to worry, become a professional one like the efficiency expert. That way you'll not only get paid for worrying about troubles, but they'll also be someone else's!

Any action you take to solve a problem will relieve your mind for you'll be actively doing something to change the status quo. Even if it's wrong, you'll feel better because you're doing something about it (at least, you'll get an E for effort!). Once you get going, you'll find your mind will start to click. Your imagination will loosen up; you'll be stimulated to find new ways to solve your problems. Dig into the situation; you'll get a better understanding of it. That's why so many of your best ideas come when you're actively working on your problems.

Learn from others   Why do most of us insist on learning everything the hard way? Trial and error methods are costly and inefficient. Profit from the successes and failures of other people.

The library is full of books on self-improvement. A library card costs nothing. When you find a book you want to underline and make a permanent part of your reference library like this one, then it's time to buy it.

You can tell if you're really trying to learn from others or not, simply by looking at some of the books you've read to improve yourself. In many cases, you'll find that the first four or five chapters will be underlined and have notes along the margin; the rest of the book will be clean. Did the author run dry, or did you run out of steam and quit?

In either case, it's about like trying to build a house without a hammer and a saw. Learning shouldn't end when you leave school; that's when it usually starts!

Don't wait for inspiration to strike   Most people think you must be in the right mood before you can accomplish anything worth while. That's not true. Two plus two always equals four for the happy mathematician as well as for the sad one. Moods have nothing to do with it. If something is disagreeable or boring to you, and you wait for inspiration, chances are you'll never be inspired to go to work on it.

"Successful Ideas Are 2% Inspiration—98% Perspiration," is a chapter title in one of my books, *Guide to Managing People*.* "Every invention, from the first crude wheel to the intricate and highly sophisticated control system of a manned space rocket, had its beginning in the dark caverns of the mind. Almost every major innovation you can name came into existence because *a persistent man with an idea wouldn't give up*. That's why successful ideas are only 2 percent inspiration and 98 percent perspiration."

Work up a self-monitoring system   It isn't enough to check on yourself when the job's about to be finished. If you wait until then to make your first check, it's usually too late. Use a series of checkpoints. For instance, if you want to see fifty prospects by the end of the week, you better check yourself out on Tuesday and Thursday to see where you stand. If you wait until Friday noon, it's too late; your week's completely shot.

"Our salesmen all work on a straight commission basis," says J. J. Bollinger, president of the Doctors Health and Hospital Insurance

---

* James K. Van Fleet, *Guide to Managing People* (Parker Publishing Company, Inc., 1968).

Company, Des Moines, Iowa. "I always tell them the week might not be over until Friday night, but they sure ought to know where they stand by Wednesday. The week's more than half gone by then; if they're just starting to warm up, it's getting right late. Time runs out fast for a salesman on Thursday and Friday!"

Establish deadlines   Besides using a self-monitoring system, another good way to commit yourself is to set exact time limits for getting things done. There's a lot of difference between saying "I'll answer his letter first chance I get," and "I'll answer his letter before I go home tonight."

When you establish deadlines, watch for these two points:

1. Make them realistic.
2. Stick to them.

Make note-taking a habit   It's ridiculous to miss a $250 sale if you forgot an appointment because you wouldn't spend 25¢ for a notebook. Don't pride yourself on your memory. You can be proud of so many other accomplishments. (An army officer without a notebook and pencil is more likely to be court-martialed than one who forgets to carry his weapon!)

If you think note taking is a waste of time, let me ask you this: How many good ideas have you *never* tried out? Why not? I'll bet you forgot 'em; that's why!

Insist to yourself that you get started   If you're like the rest of us, you associate confidence with action and a lack of confidence with no action. You can increase confidence in yourself by forcing yourself to take some action. Once you start doing something, your self-confidence automatically goes up. You'll find you can change your feelings by first changing your actions.

Fight off purposeful forgetting   The tendency to forget what you don't want to remember is so strong that psychologists call it "purposeful forgetting." That's why we bury the bad things of the past and remember only the good times.

A reformed drunk tells funny stories about his drinking days, but he never mentions the car wrecks. When old soldiers get together, they never reminisce about death and sorrow. In fact, they never talk about fighting. They talk only about the wine and the women of France and Japan!

You can fight off this problem of purposeful forgetting if you—

1. Make definite, concrete, and specific plans.
2. Fix deadlines for getting things done.
3. Set up a system to check yourself out.
4. Keep records of what you do.
5. Analyze your records so you can correct your mistakes.

Start off each day with a success experience   I'm sure you've heard people say, "Something happened this morning that ruined my whole day." If this is really true, that person might as well have turned around and gone back home to bed. Somehow I doubt that his whole day was completely ruined. I think maybe he just had a bad ten minutes that morning, but he nursed it all day!

If you usually feel tops early in the morning, this is the best time to tackle the hardest thing you need to do. However, if you're like most of us, you need a little time to "warm up." If so, then you'd best start off with something you're sure won't go sour on you.

Clearly distinguish between plans and goals   Most salesmen are always trying to figure out new ways to sell more. An aggressive life insurance agent might say, "I plan to write $50,000 worth of business next month." Is this a plan or a goal? Actually, he's only stated his goal. He might not have any plan at all about how he's going to do it. The obvious answer is for him to make up a specific plan that will show how he's going to reach his goal of $50,000.

There's a difference between knowing and doing   For instance, let's say you're a Kenmore salesman who knows five different closing methods, but you're only using one. You're no better off than the salesman who knows only one. If you think you need improvement in some area, figure out what you're using, and look for new methods that can be useful to you.

Cultivate your use of time   Get in the habit of putting a mental price on your time; you'll gain new respect for it. Such an approach will also help you decide whether it's really worthwhile to tackle many of the minor jobs that are now eating a hole in your working day. You can better manage your time if you will——

1. Learn to say "No."
2. Avoid telephone traps.
3. Discourage interruptions.
4. Listen.
5. Do it right now.
6. Do it right the first time.
7. Do it only once.
8. Use all the time you have.
9. Anticipate your daily needs.

Learn to say "No"   If you don't learn to say "No," you'll find yourself beseiged by all kinds of do-gooders. You'll be lured into doing things and going places you don't want to. Remember, charity begins at home, so be good to yourself for a change. Learn to say "No!"

Now I'm not saying do-gooders don't have their place. They do. But I've also seen some real fine people turn into bears because of too heavy commitments to PTA, Boy and Girl Scouts, Red Cross, Community Fund, church and social activities, etc. You can't save the whole world all by yourself, so why try?

Avoid telephone traps   I'm not suggesting that you write a letter when a phone call would be quicker. You can't beat the phone as a time saving device to get information, order supplies, clear up misunderstandings, issue instructions, and make appointments.

But it's also an easy way to waste time through pointless gossip, social chatter, and the like. And men are as guilty as women. Protect yourself and your time by knowing beforehand what you want to say

. . . what you want to do . . . with whom you want to speak . . .
the telephone numbers you want to reach. Then keep your calls on a
businesslike basis.

Discourage interruptions   Well-meaning friends and business
associates just shooting the breeze can throw your best-planned day
for a complete loss. You can keep their friendship—and your schedule
—if you let them know in a decent way that you're pushed for time.
It's a lot easier to shoot the breeze and have coffee call in a real estate
office than it is to buckle down and make some phone calls to prospective buyers or sellers, but it's not as profitable.

Some men face the wall or work with their backs to others. Some
juggle their lunch hours around so they can work while others are
eating. Wayne Parker, one of the most successful men I've ever met
in the real estate business, has a sign on his desk that makes the point
quite well, I think, for it says—*"If you have nothing to do—don't do
it here!"*

I, too, am very blunt. I do most of my work at home in a room
that acts as a den, an office, and a library. Most of the time my wife
answers the phone and the door. I refuse all phone calls and I'll see
no one between 9:00 and 3:00. If I do get stuck once in a while and
one of those door-to-door salesmen show up while she's gone, I simply
tell them what my time is worth per hour. Then I ask them how much
they'd like to buy—fifteen minutes, half an hour, or an hour's worth.
I don't get too many takers!

Listen   You can save all sorts of costly mistakes, backtrack-
ing, and doing things over if you get instructions and information right
the first time. Before you act, make sure you have *all* the facts. If
you're in doubt, *ask*.

Do it right now   It's human nature to put things off; it's also
unproductive. Once you know what's to be done, do it as soon as you
can. You can lick the habit of putting things off. That's what this
chapter is all about—showing you how to become your own self-

starter so you can get those things done that will give you power with people.

Do it right the first time   Plenty of rehearsals will insure success when it's time for the real thing. People hate lifeboat drills, but without dry runs a lot of lives can be lost when it turns out to be a wet run. Do it right the first time; you'll save time.

Do it only once   E. Joseph Cossman, mail-order millionaire, says this in his book, *How I Made $1,000,000 in Mail Order* *: "Look at each piece of correspondence, think about it, make a decision, pass it along for action, file it, or destroy it . . . *but never, never handle the same piece of paper twice.* Your fidelity to this rule will keep your desk clear."

After reading Mr. Cossman's words, I put his rule to work. I've added nearly two hours to my working day. It's a hard rule to live by, but it can be done. The amount of time you gain is well worth the pain of improving your memory banks.

Use all the time you have   You can really add to your productive hours if you'll use every single minute you're awake. This means using all your travel time, your waiting time, your eating time, every single minute for thinking out problems . . . planning . . . reading . . . jotting down ideas.

"In my twenty years service, I think I spent fifteen of it standing in a chow line, a pay line, a theater line, a PX line, or a latrine line," says retired army Sergeant Major Vince Reed, now a teacher in Kansas City, Missouri. "The first five years I just stood. The next ten I used that spare time to get both my bachelor's and my master's from the University of Maryland in their army overseas program."

Doctor Fred Maxwell, a St. Louis pediatrician, tells me he learned every page of Gray's Anatomy while riding the streetcar between Washington University and Florissant, a St. Louis suburb. If you're a commuter, either train or car pool, you can use that travel

* E. Joseph Cossman, *How I Made $1,000,000 in Mail Order* (Englewood Cliffs, N.J., Prentice-Hall, Inc., 1963).

time profitably, or you can stare blankly out the window. It's all up to you.

Anticipate your daily needs   This one sounds so simple I know you'll laugh when you first read it. But please try it; you'll soon stop laughing. I did.

You can avoid those minor, time-wasting, nail-chewing frustrations that whittle away your time and your temper by looking ahead and planning for those little daily crises.

You should have on hand such simple everyday items as small change for the parking meter, the coffee machine, and the cigarette machine; stamps, paper clips, rubber bands, stationery, etc. If necessary, have duplicates of your keys, shoelaces, glasses, umbrellas, handkerchiefs, comb, electric razor, at the office as well as your home. (My wife says this list should include lipstick, perfume, and hose; I bow to her feminine judgment.) Decide the night before what you're going to wear the next day and lay it out then.

All this boils down to simple prior planning for the basics of earning a living. It's a lot like making up the grocery list or paying the monthly bills, not exciting, but required. And it should become so routine for you it's second nature. Then you won't waste time thinking about it.

POINTS TO REMEMBER

Gaining the benefits

To gain the benefits of never being caught off guard by your competitors or your enemies, building a reputation for getting things done, and not missing the opportunity for promotion or advancement, use these techniques:

(1) Pin-point your goal by (2) making a list of everything that needs to be done and (3) put that list right in front of you. Then you

can (4) concentrate on the essentials. Do that and it's much easier to (5) re-sell yourself on the benefits you'll gain.

If you (6) give yourself a small part of the job to do, it's easier to (7) work up a written step-by-step plan (8) along with some alternate plans. This way, you can more easily (9) reach a decision that will (10) emphasize doing rather than doing perfectly.

If you want to (11) figure out why you're putting things off, (12) get your problems down on paper. Then you can (13) use your energy for action and not for worrying.

(14) Don't wait for inspiration to strike while you're in deep meditation (worrying?), but scurry around and work up a little sweat by (15) learning from others.

You can (16) work up a self-monitoring system by (17) establishing deadlines, (18) making note-taking a habit, and (19) insisting to yourself that you get started so you can (20) fight off purposeful forgetting.

(21) Start each day with a success experience; you'll soon be able to (22) clearly see the difference between goals and plans, and thus realize (23) knowing and doing are not the same thing.

Time is one of your most valuable assets. You can (24) cultivate its use when you (25) use every waking minute for some useful activity, (26) anticipate your daily needs, (27) learn to say "No!", (28) avoid telephone traps, (29) discourage interruptions, (30) listen so you'll get it right the first time, (31) do it immediately, (32) and do it right the first time so you'll only need to (33) do it once.

6

How to Use the Five Keys of Control

Much has been written and said about how to use the carrot and the stick, reward and punishment, money and fear to control people. Perhaps all these methods have a certain value, but their use is strictly limited. For instance, if you use fear—if you have to threaten a person with the loss of his job or demotion—you'll not inspire him to do his best for you. To tell the truth, if you have to threaten him to get him to work, he's not really worth keeping around, is he?

Now there's nothing wrong with your offering tangible rewards for exceptional efforts. But money, or incentive motivation, also has certain limitations. If you use it, *and nothing else,* to control people, you'll soon find yourself defeated by the law of diminishing returns. For as his needs are progressively satisfied, his demands will become weaker.

But let's say you can't even use money as a control measure in your own particular set up. That's all right; don't worry about it. There is a way you can control people no matter who they are or what they do. It used to be an extremely common method to use, but in these days of scientific and technological advances, shorter hours and higher salaries, fringe benefits and early retirement, this principle of control has almost disappeared. To some people, it's become so old-fashioned and out-of-date, they've almost forgotten the meaning of the term. And to many, it's a dirty four-letter word: *W-O-R-K!*

In other words, you can control others easily when you learn that you can *rule people by work and not work people by rules.* Old-fashioned or not, this principle really works.

When you know how to rule by work, and not by rules——

YOU'LL GAIN THESE BENEFITS

You'll be able to go for the maximum; you won't have to settle for the minimum

Busy people with meaningful work to do don't have time to hatch up trouble. When everyone has a worthwhile job to do and concentrates on doing it, you can fix your attention on your goal. You won't have to waste time on unnecessary discipline. You see, people who work by rules have to concentrate on dishing out discipline to those who break those rules. But people who rule by work can focus their eyes on the job to be done—the mission to be accomplished.

Just keep this thought in mind. Anybody can get the minimum from people. It takes skill, know-how, and a deep understanding of human nature to get the maximum from them.

People will do what you want them to do

When you rule by work and not by rules, people will want to do what *you* want them to do. And getting people to do what you want them to do is a definite and concrete benefit you'll gain when you know how to properly control them. In fact, that benefit's the name of the game: *Power with People.* Now they'll want to do what you want them to do *just as long as they get what they want while they're doing it.* But you must retain complete command at all times. Never let them get into the driver's seat.

For instance, when you control your car, it goes where you want it to go. When it's out of control, it goes where it wants to go. But people out of control are worse than any runaway car. They can think and plot and scheme—a car cannot!

Another big benefit

Here's another big benefit you'll gain from the proper control of people—When you can achieve that second benefit of getting people to want to do what you want them to do, making sure they'll get what they want while they're doing it, you'll automatically gain this benefit: You'll have people who'll respect you and have confidence in you; people who will give you their willing obedience, loyal cooperation, and full support.

And that, my friend, is real control of people. I know some mighty rich men—and women, too—who'd give an arm or a leg to have influence like that, but they can't buy it in spite of all their money. Even the President of the United States, sitting in the most powerful elected position in the entire world, cannot buy that kind of control of people. It's just not for sale at any price.

But you can get that kind of control with people, and it won't cost you a dime. Just remember this one simple principle: *Rule by work—don't work by rules*. And now for the——

TECHNIQUES YOU CAN USE
TO PUT THIS PRINCIPLE TO WORK AND
GAIN THE BENEFITS

Some of these techniques might sound familiar to you old-timers. But if you're strictly cybernetics minded and computer trained, they'll no doubt sound quite strange. But familiar or strange, old or new, they will work for you and that's the important thing. I know that IBM says machines should work and people should think, but I also know this: *Technicians work only with things; executives work with people*.

But enough. You get my idea, I'm sure. Now for the techniques.

THE FIVE KEYS OF CONTROL

1. Give everyone a specific job to do; get 'em all involved.
2. Organize your people so you can best exercise control of them.
3. To supervise people properly—use the correct span of control.
4. To control people—decentralize responsibility.
5. To lead and control people—you must first be a leader.

And now in detail from the top down. . . .

Give everyone a specific job to do; get them all involved

When you give people something *worthwhile and meaningful* to do, something that'll keep them physically as well as mentally occupied, they'll be happy and contented with their work. And this technique works for ministers as well as for anyone else, that is, if they understand the principle of application as well as Reverend Price Jennings does.

"Get him involved. Give him a job to do," says Reverend Jennings, pastor of the Brentwood Hills Christian Church in Independence, Missouri. "Most ministers complain they can't keep young people between 18 and 30 interested in the church.

"You know why? They don't give them a job to do; that's why. Religion is made up of two W's—*Worship* and *Work*. And they must be properly balanced. You can't keep young people coming with too much preaching from me and too little work from them.

"Young people are interested in developing a better world. And they know they can't do it with just a couple of hymns, a prayer, and a sermon on Sunday morning. They know that worship alone, important as it might be, just isn't enough. It takes a lot of work, too.

"Our church is crammed and overflowing with young men and women because we offer them participation—not substitution. The goal of our youth activity program is to make better the communities we live in. So we worship in the church; we work in our neighborhoods.

"A Christmas and Thanksgiving basket for the poor family is not the answer. It takes much more than that. For instance, I watched Charles Kuralt, the traveling CBS newsman, report on how people in Las Vegas, Nevada, got together and built a much needed city park in a poor neighborhood in just about 24 hours.

"How'd they do it? Well, everybody, young and old, rich and poor, black and white, Catholic and Protestant, pitched in and helped. Everybody had a job to do and they did it. That's how. That's the kind of thing I mean."

You can use this same approach on Junior If you're a father or mother and your children have reached the walking and talking stage, I'm sure you'll readily recognize this scene:

It's a rainy Sunday afternoon. John and Sue, Mr. and Mrs. Adams, that is, and their only child, a ten-year-old, John, Junior, have all been to church, eaten their Sunday dinner out, and are all back home again. John, Senior, has settled down in front of the fireplace with the Sunday sports section. Sue has stretched out on the davenport for just a "five-minute" nap. But John, Junior, isn't about to be pleased so easily. After wandering aimlessly around the house for a few minutes, back he comes to his father.

"Dad, can I go over to Larry's house for a while? Or how about let's you and me go take in a movie? Or let's go look at campers and travel trailers . . . or boats . . . or something. Say, why can't we drive down to the lake, Dad? I'll bet it's not even raining down there . . . but Dad . . . *I've got nothing to do!*"

Your kids need something worthwhile to do, too That's right. They need a meaningful and worthwhile job to do that will keep them physically and mentally occupied and give them a sense of accomplishment when their work is finished. And it takes more than ping-pong or billiards in the rec room to get the job done, and we enjoy both of them, too.

You say Susie doesn't like to cook? How do you know? Have you ever given her the chance, or do you keep her out of the kitchen because she makes too much of a mess? Just washing or drying the dishes won't fetch it!

How about Junior? Does he have a mechanical ability? Get him a carpenter's set or a mechanic's tool kit or whatever is needed to develop his natural talents. My youngest son spends hours in the garage disassembling and assembling his mini-bike.

Sure, it's hard to figure out how to keep a child physically occupied all the time, but it's the key to keeping him out of trouble, too. Find out which of the nine subconscious desires is the most dominant one and give him the chance to fulfill it. (You learned how to become your own intelligence agent back in Chapter 2. Remember? Now it's time to put your newly acquired knowledge to work.) In a child, it's usually a creative desire that's demanding fulfillment. It's up to you to find out what those natural talents of his are and help him develop them.

You say you want to learn how to gain power with people—not study child psychology? I've got good news for you. When you can succeed in keeping your children occupied and happy and busy, you're close to being an expert. When you can do that, you're ready for the big time outside. Of course, if you use force and fear to get the job done at home, that doesn't count. You're not playing the game at all that way.

Organize your people
so you can best exercise control over them

No matter how small your group is, or how minor the work to be done, if you have two or more people in the group, someone has to be the boss. Someone has to assume the mantle of leadership and take charge if anything at all is to get done.

So you need some sort of organization, no matter how loose it is. The more complex the group and the more detailed the work to be done—the better must be your organization for the control of people.

"The organization of your group has a marked influence on your desired results," says Dr. Harvey Watson, head of Drury College's Psychology Department. "And the more people you have to control, the more skillful must be your methods and your approach.

"For instance, if you, as an employer, have only two employees, you will have two human relationships—one with each one of your employees. But that isn't all. Each of these relationships between you and your subordinates will be influenced and modified by a third relationship, the one that exists between your two employees.

"And the more employees you have, the more complex will be the results of these various interacting relationships, and the more difficult will be your problems of people control.

"That problem isn't confined to the employer-employee relationship either. I have it right here in the teacher-student complex in the classroom. You'll find it between Boy Scout leaders and their troops; between football coaches and their teams; preachers and their congregations; parents and their children.

"In short, you'll always find it wherever two or more persons get together. One person will always become the leader; the rest will always become followers. It always works that way."

If you're the leader of your group, then the relationships created between you and your people should be designed to increase your own effectiveness as that leader. To help you achieve that goal, I want to give you now the *Principles of Organization for Control of People:*

ESSENTIALITY. Each part of your organization should be needed to accomplish your mission or it should not exist. If it's not absolutely necessary to do the job—get rid of it. Nice to have doesn't belong here.

BALANCE. Each section of your organization should be designed to do its part of the job properly, but without duplication of the efforts of any of your other sections.

COORDINATION. You should have the group members coordinate and cooperate with each other to keep from having either gaps or overlaps in the work.

FLEXIBILITY. Your organization should be designed to perform its mission without interruption even though the job might change in scope or final objective.

EFFICIENCY. You should make the best use possible of people, money, materials, facilities, and time without undue waste of any of them.

Now that you know the principles of organization for the control of people, I'd now like to take up the actual organizing process itself. The organizing process is made up of three distinct parts:

1. Determination of the basic task to be done.
2. Setting up the organizational structure to do that task.
3. Allocation of resources to the various people, sections, or departments, etc.

Determine the task to be done   The job as a whole must be specified, whether it be to put up a pup tent or to build a skyscraper. Then that job should be divided into the various functions that are to be performed. When a complete list of these operations has been made, group the related tasks together for assignment to the proper people.

Set up the structure to do that task   This is the second step in the organizing process. Its completion will usually end up in the creation of an organizational chart, no matter how simple. Your chart should show graphically how each element of your group is related to the other elements. It should also show the chain through which authority passes.

Allocate the resources   This is your last step. Military units are usually given their physical resources by a table or organization and equipment. Such a table shows what personnel and equipment the leader will have to work with. Highly complex organizations like General Motors, Ford, General Electric, Westinghouse, etc., are all organized in much the same way.

More informal organizations where people are often unpaid volunteers also use these same basic principles of organization to get the job done. You can use Boy Scout work; Little League; Junior Chamber of Commerce; a local safety council; a civic club, fraternal lodge, or church committee work to gain a good education and solid experience in the art of organizing to control people and get a specific job done.

Now I did want to give you a practical example of how the organizing process can be used, so I wrote to Jim Henderson the other day and asked him for some help on this. Jim is the president and general manager of his own general contracting firm in St. Louis, Missouri. I asked him to do this for two main reasons: First of all, he's a highly successful contractor. Secondly, I know of no other business in the world that requires more painstaking organizing ability and know-how than the general contracting and construction business.

Here's what Jim said in his letter to me:

" *'How to Keep from Going Broke in the Contracting Business'* should be the title of this letter," says Jim. "It's an old, old saying in the contracting and construction business that the successful contractor is the one who hasn't gone broke yet!

"My methods of operation or my organization for business follows a pattern like this:

"1. I collect and keep current and up-to-date detailed data on all construction costs.

"2. I surround myself with experts in a variety of fields for I find that I often need help in such specialized areas as engineering, financing, purchasing, taxation, law, etc. Some of these people are permanent members of my corporation. Others work on a consulting basis only as needed.

"3. I have competent foremen and supervisors and I pay them well to keep them. Only with their top-notch assistance can I keep my labor turnover down. Because of their efforts I'm able to maintain good working labor relations with all my men.

"4. I buy only the best equipment and I keep it running through a positive and definite program of inspection, maintenance, and operator training.

"5. I make allowances for such conditions as storms, weather, temperature, seasons, floods, climate, and other problems in my estimates and my plans.

"6. I use the most economical methods of construction possible, but without any sacrifice of quality.

"7. That's why I have an inspection section that's second to none I found out long ago that quality control is a big outfit's worst headache. It's their job to insure that quality control that I must have to stay in business.

"8. My production superintendent, Henry Jackson, acts as my coordinator and direct representative in timing and programming a project. He takes care of the flow of materials to the construction site at the proper time, in the right amount, with correct specifications and proper quality, so that nothing will be overlooked and work will not be delayed costing me money because of a penalty clause.

"He works in close conjunction with my quality control section to insure acceptance by the customer so I won't be hit with costly adjustments or doing part of the project over. I couldn't do without Henry. He's my right-hand man.

"9. I also have a progress and costs department where accurate records are kept to show whether any particular project is ahead of schedule, behind schedule, or right on the money. They also keep detailed costs and other statistical data so that my next bid on a contract will be sure to cover the continually rising costs of inflation. I can't afford to build something on my own money!

"Now my methods may not be exactly like those that other contractors use, but I'll bet you this. If he's been in business for 10 years or more, and still going, I'd be safe in saying that our methods are almost identical!"

To supervise people properly—
use the correct span of control

The span of control is the number of immediate subordinates one person can control, supervise, and direct effectively. If more effective control of people is your primary goal, you should understand thoroughly the span of control and the factors that can affect and influence it.

One of these factors is the *span of attention*. That is, the ability of a person to divide his attention between two or more tasks. Each one of us has an upper limit beyond which we cannot give our attention to any more work, no matter how pressing or how important it is. Even below this upper limit, assignment of any new job tends to detract from the efficient accomplishment of those tasks already at hand. Not only that, our ability to divide attention decreases as mental or physical exhaustion increases. So the maximum span of control diminishes rapidly with increased mental or physical fatigue.

Another factor that affects the span of control stems from the individual attitudes of people. If you have a predetermined and set point of view, your ability to reason logically is impaired. Take jury duty, for instance; if a prospective juror has already formed an opinion about the guilt or innocence of the defendant, he cannot be allowed to serve on the jury. If you have a predetermined view, you can easily misinterpret or misunderstand what you see and hear. You'll tend to make this information fit your preconceived opinion. Such a biased attitude can affect your ability to control people effectively.

"Don't violate the span of control," says William Hartline, the president of Republic Lumber Company, a chain of building supply centers. "As long as you don't violate the span of control, the total number of people you employ or control has little or no actual bearing on your ability to lead and supervise people. The span of control is the number of *immediate subordinates* that one person can control, supervise, or direct effectively.

"Most management consultants feel that the economically minimum span of control is three. Give a man less than three immediate subordinates to supervise, and he'll have too little to do; you'll not be getting your money's worth from him.

"They also set the maximum span of control for the average

person at eight immediate subordinates. If that number is exceeded, your setup will become clumsy and hard to manage. Efficiency will go downhill.

"The number of immediate subordinates is the key to the span of control," Mr. Hartline goes on to say. "That is the key to knowing how to control large numbers of employees. For instance, you could easily control eight-hundred employees through *eight immediate subordinates.*

"You see, those eight immediate subordinates of yours will in turn have eight immediate subordinates of their own to help them establish their controls over people. When you've superimposed that span of control over your entire organization, from the top clear down to the bottom, graphically it would look like a pyramid or a triangle with you standing all alone at the very top. University, corporation, government bureau, army division—it's all the same.

"For example, in Republic Lumber, we have 125 separate building supply centers. I have five regional directors who are responsible to me for the proper operation of those centers. Each region is broken down into five districts with a chief at the head of each one. So the set up looks like this:

"A district chief has five stores in his district to control. Each store has its own separate manager, of course, with their own employees. The regional director has five district chiefs under him, so he really has twenty-five stores under his jurisdiction.

"Each regional director reports directly to me. I have a staff here in the office of three immediate subordinates so that gives me a total of eight people I personally supervise. Yet our total employee strength in the entire chain numbers just under a thousand.

"I still control that number properly for my span of control has remained constant at no more than eight—the maximum number of immediate subordinates any person should be asked to handle. It's at the lower levels where I have to beef up the number of supervisory personnel to take care of the load.

"I do know that whenever companies and corporations are having problems of communication and control, you'll always find they're violating this span of control.

"And although I'm not an army man, I did spend a couple of years in service, and I think I know enough about people to say with a definite degree of certainty that the same problem exists in there as out here."

Now in view of what Mr. Hartline says about the span of control and how important it is in the proper supervision and control of people, I asked him to help me make up a checklist for you so you could evaluate your own people control problems. If you are having problems of control, it could well be that you might find your answer right here:

Factors That Will Influence
the Upper Limit of Your Span of Control

1. Your own individual experience, background, and training.
2. The experience, background, and training of your people.
3. The amount of *clearly understood* communication between you and your subordinates.
4. The degree of similarity of your subordinates' jobs.
5. The distance that physically separates you and your subordinates.
6. The time normally available to translate your desires into action.
7. Your own personality and the personality of each of your people.
8. The mental and physical condition of you and your subordinates.
9. The complexity of your organization structure.

To control people—
decentralize responsibility

It sometimes comes as a shock to a high-level executive to find out that to get more work out of people and to control them better, he must give them even more to do; that is, he must relinquish the tight reins of authority. In short, he must give a person a job to do and then he must give him the authority to do it.

Delegation of authority is not an easy thing to come by. The idea of handing over a job to someone else to do—one that you know perfectly well you can do as well, if not better, yourself—goes against the grain. But unless you do, you'll have to do all the work yourself.

But the day of the one-man show is nearly finished. Choosing a top man to help you can be vitally important to your success. Remember how Jim Henderson said he couldn't do without Henry Jackson; how Henry was his right-hand man? Maybe you could use some help like that, too. I can give you three solid reasons why you need to develop a good assistant to help you if you're in business for yourself:

1. *He takes part of the work load off your shoulders.* This will give you more time for your other management duties. He can make your job easier for you by giving you time to plan, to think, and to meet emergencies.

2. *He can step into your shoes and keep the business going.* Maybe you've never been sick a single day in your life. But sooner or later that day will come. The law of averages will catch up with you. What will you do if you have an accident and no one's trained to take your place? Suppose you break an arm or a leg? What then? Can your wife or your husband take over and run the show?

3. *You can take some time off for play.* A vacation's a necessary breather. With a competent and trusted assistant, you can take time away from your business to do things with your family and your friends. The right man, properly trained, can help you live a fuller life both at work and at home.

To decentralize responsibility—use the break-even point   "So many times, I find a supervisor doing the job a production employee should be doing," says James F. Dwyer, a department foreman with Allied Chemical Company. "When I ask that supervisor why he's doing work that rightfully belongs to someone else, he says, 'It takes me longer to explain how to do it to someone than it takes me to do it myself!'

"Now that may be true, but it should be true only once. The fallacy of his reasoning lies in the fact that although it might take him fifteen minutes to explain the job he wants done to the employee, and only five minutes to do the job himself, he'll have to explain it only once if he does it properly.

"When the employee has done the job just three times—then the supervisor has reached the *breakeven point*. From then on he's ahead of the game. He can devote his time to something else that he should be doing."

To control people—
you must first be a leader

I suppose that it goes without saying that you couldn't be a leader unless you had some followers. As Mark Twain once said, "We should be thankful for the indolent, since without them the rest of us could not get ahead." Since this is true, you might think I should have covered this point at the beginning of the chapter. I didn't want to, because being a leader is quite demanding and I did not want to discourage you. Anyway, whether it's first or last is just a matter of relativity.

To get ahead with other people, you must be a leader and that's a fact. It's an essential. There are five primary character traits you must have if you want to develop your ability to lead and to control other people. These specific attributes are——

1. Character.
2. The power of decision.
3. The wisdom to plan and order.
4. The courage to act.
5. The capacity to manage.

Seldom in this book have I been arbitrary in my statements. However, this is the one time that I will be. Although I know leaders are not born, but made, still I also know that these five primary traits must be pronounced characteristics in a person if he is to lead others. If even one is noticeably lacking, that person will not succeed as a leader. But if all are present, he *can* develop into an excellent leader of people.

These, then, are the specific characteristics people look for when they are selecting their leaders, or when they are looking for someone to promote to higher responsibilities in leadership or management— Please mark them well:

Character is your first essential trait   If you have character, you will instinctively know the difference between right and wrong. Not only do you know the right thing to do, but you also have the courage to do it. You will be a person of honor. You are to be trusted. You will not lie, cheat, or steal, no matter what advantage would be gained by doing so.

You must possess the power of decision   You must be able to make a decision. It is not enough that you use logic and reasoning in making an estimate of the situation. Many people can do that. But a rare few have the strength of character it takes to make that decision at the right time and then announce it without hesitation. Today's problems will never be solved with tomorrow's solutions.

You need the wisdom to plan and order   Once you make your decision, you must develop a workable plan to carry it out. Definite and specific tasks must be given to your people. Your plan must answer certain specific questions: What is to be done? Who will do it? Where will it be done, when, and how? The wisdom to plan and order is one of the essential characteristics that you will need if you want to lead and control other people.

You must have the courage to act   Even though you have the power of making sound decisions, and of making excellent plans and orders based upon those decisions, you will still be far from gaining your goals unless you have the courage to act. The brilliant thinker with the faint heart invites only disaster through his inaction or his hesitancy to move. You must have the courage to do what has to be done, despite the costs, the hardships, the hazards, and the sacrifices.

Though you have vision to see what needs to be done and the wisdom of Solomon to help you in making those decisions, you'll not influence the end result of the action unless you have the courage to act when action is required.

You must have the capacity to manage   To be a leader of others, you must develop the capacity to manage. The capacity to manage is the systematic approach to the attainment of specific goals. It requires administrative skill and know-how. Management is a tool of good leadership.

It's quite easy to take the perfect combination of abundant and well-trained manpower, all the desired supplies and equipment, unlimited funds, and indefinite time to complete a project. That's no challenge at all; anyone can do that! The real challenge to your management ability comes when you have to make the best use of whatever you have on hand to get what you want. You'll be measured more by what you get done under such circumstances than by what you do.

POINTS TO REMEMBER

One principle to follow is: *Rule by work—don't work by rules.*

Three benefits you'll gain
1. You can go for the maximum; you won't have to settle for the minimum.
2. People will do what you want them to do.
3. People will respect you and have confidence in you; they'll give you their willing obedience, loyal cooperation, and full support.

Techniques to use: the five keys of control
1. Give everyone a specific job to do; get 'em all involved.
2. Organize your people so you can best exercise control of them.

3. To supervise people properly—use the correct span of control.
4. To control people—decentralize responsibility.
5. To lead and control people—you must first be a leader.

7

How to Use
Security and Surprise
to Gain Success with People

The use of security to keep your plans and intentions clothed in secrecy will allow you to take your competitor by surprise. Security and surprise go together like pork chops and applesauce. They make up the right combination of success just like the deadly one-two punch of the professional boxer. That's why I've put them together in this chapter. They just naturally belong with each other.

Back in Chapter Two, if you will recall, we talked about how to mount your own intelligence effort to gain information about two specific kinds of people. These two kinds were:

1. The people who could help you reach your goals and become successful.
2. Those people who could harm you or prevent you from attaining your objectives.

Although the material in all previous chapters is applicable to both types of people, up to now I have concentrated primarily on the first kind—those who could help you become successful. In this chapter, I'm going to take up the second kind of people—those who could harm you or those who could prevent you from reaching your goals. The descriptive terms I use here will be primarily *enemy, opponent, competitor.*

Let me clear up one point now, if you will, just in case there's any confusion in your mind. Your intelligence efforts to gather information about other people is called *positive intelligence.* (The CIA would call it *espionage.* That's the kind we covered in Chapter 2.) The efforts you make to keep your enemy from gathering information about you would be called *counter-intelligence.* That's the kind we'll cover now.

Security, then, is counter-intelligence— not positive intelligence

Security takes in all the active measures you use to keep your intentions and your plans, your actions and your movements, a complete secret from others so you can take them by complete surprise.

By breaching our security, and by keeping their plans a secret, the Japanese surprised the United States forces and caught them completely off guard at Pearl Harbor. General MacArthur veiled his plans in absolute secrecy to surprise the North Koreans by the Inchon landings.

Even as far back as 500 B.C., the Chinese warrior Sun-tzu said, "He will win who, prepared himself, waits to take the enemy unprepared."

Now the benefits of using security and surprise have remained much the same over the years since Sun-tzu made that statement. Even the basic techniques have changed but little. They are the same except, perhaps, for technological and scientific refinements, for man himself has not changed throughout those years. His basic needs and desires remain the same.

BENEFITS YOU'LL GAIN
BY USING SECURITY AND SURPRISE

You won't tip your hand

Use proper security and you'll benefit by not tipping your hand to your competitor. Clothe your plans and your intentions, your actions and your movements, with complete secrecy. Even in the management of a business, the principle of security still holds true. Successful professional managers and businessmen don't tip their hand to their competitors by bragging about their successes. They don't leave notes, materials, and data lying around where just anyone could pick them up. Even the night janitor could be a spy for the opposition. Janitors are a favorite target because of their low pay and their menial duties.

Don't be fooled by TV and the movies. Sure, sex is an effective tool to use in the cloak and dagger business, but the more ordinary and common the spy appears to be, the better are his chances for success. More company secrets and confidential papers have been stolen by janitors in overalls than by torrid sexpots in panties.

You won't be taken by surprise

Your proper use of security will keep your competitor from taking you by surprise. While you must make every possible effort to surprise your enemy, it's just as important—sometimes, more so—to guard against the enemy taking you by surprise. Don't be caught off guard by carelessness and inattention.

Ordinarily, you don't have to hire a big security force and double the guard at the main gate to keep from being taken by surprise. Just remember to clean off your desk and lock your confidential documents in the safe, for instance. Don't forget the janitor and the snoopy night supervisor.

You'll surprise your opponent

When you keep your plans and your actions properly secured and secret, you'll be able to take your opponent by surprise. The principle of surprise is one of the most effective and most influential weapons to use in war. It can turn the tide of battle even when all odds are completely against you. Among the ancients, Genghis Khan, Caesar, Hannibal, and Alexander used the principle of surprise far better than most conquerors. In more modern times, surprise attacks to gain the initial advantage were used quite effectively by Japan and North Korea against the United States. Both World War II and the Korean Conflict were started by surprise attacks when we least expected them—on Sunday morning.

Your benefits exceed your effort

When you use surprise, you'll gain benefits that are all of of proportion to the efforts expended. Surprise can be achieved by *originality, audacity, speed,* and *secrecy.* In every instance, absolute and complete concealment of your intentions and speed of execution are essential. The New York Jets used all four factors—originality, audacity, speed, secrecy—to baffle the Baltimore Colts and capture football's Super Bowl Title in the AFL-NFL play-off in January 1969.

The Mustang is the classic business example of how Ford used security and secrecy to surprise all their competitors and beat them to the punch. The entire automobile industry was caught off guard. The best indication of the Mustang's success has been the number of carbon copies that followed it.

So much, then, for the benefits. Now for the techniques.

TECHNIQUES YOU CAN USE
TO GAIN THESE BENEFITS

Although security and surprise usually go hand-in-hand, for the sake of clarity, I'd like to talk about them one at a time, starting with security. Without first attaining security, you'd have but little chance of achieving surprise. To do this, and since I always like to be as specific as possible about methods and techniques, I've made up this ten-point security checklist for you.

Please keep in mind that although this checklist has been made up primarily from security check-points used in lots of businesses, and industry, too—its principles can be easily adapted to any given situation you might run into. In fact, you can use these points for take-off— once you're in the air, you can fly on your own.

SECURITY CHECKLIST

1. Consider all company business as strictly confidential.
2. Never discuss business problems outside your office—not even with your wife.
3. Never brag about your business successes to anyone.
4. Guard your company secrets as closely as you would your daughter's morals.
5. Never let employment agencies know all the details of specific jobs in your company.
6. Don't leave copies of your notes or other company documents lying around.
7. Lock all desks and file cabinets when not in use and when you go home at night.
8. Destroy all paper waste daily—*especially carbon paper.*
9. Don't reveal actual projects that are still in the developmental stages at a trade show, a fair, etc.
10. Operate on a need to know basis. Plug all possible sources of information leaks.

Consider all company business as strictly confidential

Your first step to keep your competition from learning your trade secrets, your business plans, and your projects is to keep all company business on a confidential basis. Without this approach, you'll never be able to maintain full security about your business. When your enemy (or your competition) doesn't know what your intentions are—

but when you know his—you have power over him that he doesn't have over you. It's your job to keep it that way.

Most big plants today have a guard system and a high wire fence to prevent sabotage, especially if the plant has to do with national defense. Of course, these barriers help to keep unwanted people out, but that's not enough. Your security system has to extend on inside your place to cover your own employees. The whole idea of security implies that it's essential to safeguard vital information from the opposition, be it on the outside or the inside, for to do so keeps him from gaining power over you. Withholding of important plans and keeping confidential data from enemy hands are necessary if you're going to use the tactics of surprise, and at the same time, keep him from using surprise against you.

But just because you have a high wire fence and a guard at the main gate, don't relax your security measures inside the plant. Remember this. A padlock will only keep an honest man honest; it'll not keep a real burglar out. And just because a man's on your payroll, don't assume he's automatically loyal to you. He could have been planted by the opposition.

Your best approach, then, is to consider every bit of company business as completely confidential. This doesn't mean you should go around the place playing cloak and dagger games with your employees. But it does mean that you should keep certain information within a definite closed circle. If a man needs to know something to do his job, fine—tell him. If he doesn't need to know, but insists on knowing anyway, you have a right to look at him with an eye of deep suspicion.

Never discuss business problems outside your office— not even with your wife

The rule of thumb in most outfits is never to discuss *confidential matters* outside the place. The trouble with this system is that you must decide what's classified "confidential" and what's completely unclassified and can be freely discussed. To further complicate this problem, what's routine and unclassified today can become confidential or top-secret tomorrow or vice-versa. So the best rule to follow here is to keep *business* business in the office and *personal* business at home.

Never brag about your business successes to anyone

Salesmen, technical representatives, and public relations people can often unknowingly violate this rule. It's fine to build up your company or your corporation image by telling *what* your company did, but keep the *how* locked up right where it belongs—in your head. When you brag about success, it just naturally leads to talking about methods and procedures, for your listener always wants to know how you managed to do it.

Guard your company secrets as closely as you would your daughter's morals

The chemical industry guards its precious secret refining processes, since these have not been patented to prevent disclosure through the public records of the United States Government Patent Office.

There's nothing at all secret about a patent. A patent is for the protection of rights—not for the protection of secrets. Cosmetic companies guard the secrecy of new products to keep competitive companies from getting the jump on their innovations. The formula for Coca-Cola has been kept a closely guarded secret for decades. And you couldn't get the secret recipe for Colonel Sanders's Southern Fried Chicken out of him either.

If you have people working for you who like to tip the bottle a little too much and who have a bad habit of picking up dates in cocktail lounges, don't let 'em in on closely guarded formulas or secrets. Liquor's an excellent tool to pry secrets out of someone. It's even better than sex. But when you combine the two, the end results can be disastrous to you. Rather than run the risk of losing some valuable company secrets through a tipsy employee or executive, you'd be far better off to get rid of him. If you do have to keep him, transfer him to a non-sensitive position. He might get the point and quit.

Never let employment agencies know all the details of specific jobs in your company

If you happen to use the services of an employment agency, it's enough to say that you're looking for a chemical engineer with a degree and umpteen years experience in the textile field—that's all you need to say. If you hire him, you can teach him the specific duties of his job after he's on your payroll.

Employment agencies are often entrusted with a great amount of confidential company information by careless personnel managers. This is especially true where a close relationship has developed over a long period of time. In a lot of cases, the personnel manager is only passing the buck, and letting the employment agency do all his work.

Don't leave copies of your notes or other company documents lying around

Don't ask for trouble by leaving your office for coffee or lunch without at least clearing off the top of your desk. The average subordinate simply cannot resist the temptation to take "just a quick peek" at the papers in your in-box, especially if they're hidden in a folder marked "Confidential." No matter how loyal he is, that word *confidential* acts as a green light. And just suppose he's employed by the opposition and planted in your business. Then you're really in trouble. The Minox camera makes spying easy, even for the amateur. You think it can't happen? It certainly can. It happens every day of the week to someone. It could easily happen to you.

"The spy in the corporate structure is not a myth at all," says Richard L. Sutton, head of Bell Electronics executive training and

development program. "He's very much a reality; he's for real. Your loyal, industrious man who's so anxious to learn about everybody else's job so he can get ahead in this world could really be sincere about it.

"Or he could be working for your competitor tomorrow. Maybe he's even working for him today! The piracy of trained employees and the luring of high ranking executives by other competitive companies has long been a custom in American corporate life.

"We here at Bell Electronics don't like the system one bit. We'd like to keep the people we work so hard to train, but today workers tend to look at themselves as professionals, tied not to a particular company, but to a certain skill or profession. They feel free to move, and, in fact, often do so because of their transferable skills and abilities.

"I'm not one to cry for the good old days, but I sure can remember those Studebaker ads that showed father and son working side by side in the same factory. I know they don't make Studebakers any more, but I also know they didn't fail because of organizational loyalty!"

Lock all desks and file cabinets when not in use and when you go home at night

Sure, this can be a nuisance until you get used to the idea. But to make any system work, you must work at it. Quit five minutes early and spend the last bit of the day policing up your area. People who work in Uncle Sam's Intelligence Agencies sometimes go overboard on this one, but if a secret document ever does get lost and they're at fault, they not only get their fingers slapped—but they also get their whole hand chopped off!

Destroy all paper waste daily— especially carbon paper

This can also be a nuisance—if you insist on making it one, but if security's important to you, then it's a must. It just has to be. It's one of your occupational requirements.

One way to cut down on the amount of paper waste to be destroyed is to cut down on the number of multiple copies that are generated. Go strictly on a *need to know basis*.

And always destroy the *carbon paper*. Please notice, I didn't say *carbon copies*, I said *carbon paper*. This is especially true of the throw away carbons that come in streamlined sets for an original and several copies all assembled for your convenience, but that are meant to be used only once. The carbon paper of these sets is especially legible when it's used only one time.

"A page of carbon paper gave our entire movement order to the enemy," says Dave Halprin, Chief of Counter Intelligence for the U. S. Army's Pacific Command in Honolulu. "It was back in 1953. We were moving the 19th Infantry Regiment from northern Honshu in Japan to Korea to beef up troop strength in Korea before the armistice was signed. It was supposed to be a top secret movement, but it was compromised by the enemy before our first rifle company got from Camp Haugen to Misawa Airbase.

"The old man had specified that the movement order be typed in the *exact* number of copies needed, and not mimeographed, so there'd be no chance of any extra copies flying around.

"So to comply with his commands, the troop movement orders were typed. Every single copy of the order was numbered, signed, and accounted for. But it was all a waste of time and effort. The clerk simply took the *carbon paper* and threw it in the ordinary wastepaper basket rather than putting it in the classified waste container to be burned.

"As a result of his carelessness, copies of the *top secret* troop movement order left the camp via the Japanese trash truck to fall at once into the opposition's hands!"

Don't reveal actual projects that are still in the developmental stages

In trying to build an image, capitalize on some event, or simply beat the competition to the punch, a company will sometimes unwisely authorize its public relations department or its technical representatives to release information through the press or from a speaker's platform that should've been kept secret. This may disclose your position prematurely and allow your competitor to take advantage of your untimely release of valuable information.

Operate on a need-to-know basis; plug all possible sources of information leaks

Tell me something now, if you will, please. Where but from your own competitor can you pick up skilled employees and an edge in sales and production at the same time? And how better can you avoid the high cost in time and money of training workers yourself. The answer, of course, is to get them from someone else. If you do this, so will your competitor; that's why you need a good security system to protect your interests and guard your secrets.

I know you'll never be able to completely plug every leak in the system. This is especially true when entire teams and groups of people leave. This morning I read an article by John Cunniff, a top financial columnist, about eight top-level executives who left their organization to go to work for a competitive firm in the same city.

The highest ranking member of the group was the director, executive vice-president, and general manager of an important electronics parts plant in the southwest part of the United States. Although the price of the losing firm's stock fell, and that of the gaining company went up, the corporation is big enough to weather this crisis. Could you? If you can't—better tighten up on your security. Here's one way you might do just that.

THE LITTLE PENTAGON

"When I was working in Tokyo for the U. S. Army's Intelligence Corps, I was stationed in what we called the Little Pentagon at Camp Drake," says Earl Rolfe. "Today, I use much the same system here at

Fairchild Industries in my job as the Chief of Industrial Security as we did there.

"Here at Fairchild Industries, our movements about the plant—*even as fellow employees of Fairchild*—are limited by a colored badge system. Each employee has his photograph imbedded in the badge. If you wear a green badge, you are entitled to go in all areas where the walls have a green stripe. Blue—blue; yellow—yellow; red—red, etc. A rainbow colored badge gives you the authority to enter all areas. Visitors' badges are clearly marked 'Visitor' and are also color-coded. All visitors must always be escorted.

"If you wear a green badge, for instance, you cannot go into another colored area unless you have a reason, and just like a visitor, you must be escorted. Even then, your badge entitles you to nothing more than physical movement.

"Nor does your badge give you authority to know everything that's going on even in your own department. Your access to information is still strictly on a need-to-know basis and is determined by the department head or the section chief.

"And between departments, if your job in personnel doesn't require you to know what's going on in research and development, then you aren't told. In other words, *you get to know exactly what you need to know to do your own job*. Nothing more.

"Sure, the system slows us down once in a while and people get their feelings hurt at times, but that's just part of the occupational hazard of good security. I can remember the day back in Tokyo when even the old man himself, Colonel J. B. Stanley, couldn't get into his own cryptographic room where they coded and decoded messages from Korea, Okinawa, Formosa, the Phillipines, and Honolulu. Why? He didn't have a crypto clearance!"

Now I'd like to discuss how to use surprise. Surprise is one of the most effective and powerful weapons you can use. It's a powerful tool in your campaign to achieve power with people, both in your business and your personal life. The use of surprise will bring you results that are all out of proportion to the efforts expended. This is a direct benefit of using it.

Surprise can be gained by using originality, audacity, speed, and secrecy. In every instance, success in using surprise depends upon two factors: *concealment of your true intentions and speed of execution.* There's no exception to this. It's a maxim—a truism; please keep it in mind.

In this chapter, rather than going over a list of techniques to show how to use surprise to gain your ends, I'm going to offer you a bit of variety. I want to give you a complete blow-by-blow account of how a company used both security and surprise to settle a strike, come to terms with the labor union, and gain power with people. I think this practical example will give you a better knowledge of how to use surprise.

How a company used security and surprise to end a crippling strike

A midwest company, a branch of a large eastern corporation, had been shut down tight by its failure to conclude a new contract between the company and the union. The corporation wanted to compromise over the amount of the wage increase to halt the strike as quickly as possible and cut down on lost production.

When asked for his opinion, the personnel manager at the branch plant gave the corporation president back in New York a good reason to settle the dispute quickly.

"Every day the strike goes on," he said, "the union members will become more united and more militant in their demands. The final settlement will become much more costly; it'll be extremely hard to settle with them on reasonable terms."

He also pointed out that even when the workers returned, both sides would be filled with bitterness and hatred for each other for months to come. The plant production superintendent and the industrial relations manager both agreed with the personnel manager.

The plant manager, Mr. Hoffman, wanted the strike settled, too, but only on his terms! He wanted to smash the union completely. He knew the previous plant manager had been dismissed summarily by the corporation because of his failure to produce a harmonious working relationship between the company and the union. He was thoroughly fed up with the entire labor organization and he wanted to break their back once and for all.

For the past year he'd wrangled almost daily with the union president. Ever since he'd come to Missouri to take over the plant, strike threats had hung over his head. Absenteeism was a constant headache to him. The union had become increasingly difficult to deal with on labor grievances and disputes. The arbitrator had continually ruled in favor of the union in spite of ironclad cases presented by management. He felt that a long strike now would produce labor peace and decent relations for a good many years to come.

Although Mr. Hoffman perhaps had a right to feel the way he did toward the union, the president of the corporation knew this was not the answer. He felt the plant manager was taking the wrong approach, and since so many other plants in the corporation complex were dependent upon this one plant's production, he stepped actively into the picture.

The president kept his plans and his intentions clothed tight in secrecy. Without revealing his tactics to the local plant manager, he sent his vice-president in charge of labor relations, Lloyd L. Kayser, to Missouri to take personal charge and direct the corporation strategy and tactics right on the spot.

Two days after he arrived in Missouri, Mr. Kayser caught the union completely off guard. He took them completely by surprise by running this full-page advertisement in the local newspapers. Sentiment, originally against the "out-of-town owners," immediately swung over to the side of the company.

"We're sorry our loyal employees are out on strike," the headline read.

"We're proud of our people and we hope they'll be back with us soon. Their skills and their experience have earned our company a nation-wide reputation for the finest products that money can buy.

"Our employees have treated us well and we've always tried to treat them the same way. Through their union, they have presented us with a series of wage increase requests.

"Their requests certainly seem reasonable enough and we'd like to meet them. We've always tried to pay our employees the highest wages in the rubber industry and we want to maintain that record.

"But we're sorry to say we simply can't afford to meet their current requests. Were we to do so, we'd be forced to raise the price of our products too far above our competition and the result would be less sales to our customers.

"Many other companies, all over the country, compete with us, and we must meet their prices or we will lose our present customers to them. Were that to happen, it would without question lead to fewer jobs here in our plant and greater unemployment in your city.

"Of course, we can afford to grant reasonable wage increases, and we are ready to sit down with the union to do that immediately. We'll try with your help to cut our production costs in a number of places to make up for this wage increase.

"So we hope, as we know you do, too, that this strike will end quickly for the benefit of all of us. To tell the truth, we need you, too."

Forty-eight hours after this advertisement appeared, the union members voted by an overwhelming majority to return to work. How did this happen? Why did this ad work so quickly and so effectively? There are several reasons:

The Advertisement Was Reasonable. The union had expected the company to be sullen, hard-hearted, and argumentative. This ad was a complete surprise to them for it was quiet and factual in its tone. It simply said what it had to say, and then it stopped. It calmed the troubled waters instead of stirring them up more. And without saying it in so many words, it appealed to the logic and reason and good common sense of its readers. The union had not expected this.

The Advertisement Praised the Men. Although the ad was factual, it also appealed to the proper emotions. It appealed to a man's basic emotions of loyalty and pride. The company praised the employees; it did not criticize them or degrade them in any way. This came as a complete surprise to the union.

The Ad Presented the Company Case to the Union. It did not present its case *against* the union. In most management-labor disputes, the company always presents its case *against the workers*. This time, the company presented its side *to the workers*. The union had not expected such an approach, but Mr. Kayser knew his problem was to win the union membership to his side—not to defeat them in open battle as the plant manager had so badly wanted to do.

The Ad Did Not Encourage the Union to Go Back to Work. Many companies try to split the union down the middle by encouraging a back-to-work movement. Mr. Kayser did not. Instead, he offered to sit down and negotiate immediately. Once more, he had properly interpreted the unity and the mood of the workers. So he caught them all by surprise when he made an attempt to win them over as an entire group rather than trying to split their forces into small bunches and individuals.

The Company Did Not Arbitrarily Dictate Terms. Although he was a shrewd bargainer, Mr. Kayser did not force terms down the union's throat. Instead, he left the door wide open for honorable negotiations. This allowed both the union and its bargain committee to save face, an almost unheard of procedure in management-labor relations.

Mr. Kayser Used Surprise at Every Turn. When he arrived from New York, the union assumed it was in for a fight to the death since Mr. Kayser was the vice-president in charge of labor relations for the entire corporation. In fact, the corporation's news release, prepared especially for the local newspapers by Mr. Kayser himself, hinted at the possibility of a long strike. But being the wise and seasoned negotiator that he was, Mr. Kayser kept his real intentions completely to himself, He kept his plans secret; his hand was securely hidden. When the newspaper advertisement appeared, he caught the union, *as well as the local plant management,* completely off guard for it was a complete about face from the news release!

In conclusion, I can say that Mr. Kayser's success was achieved by concealing his true intentions completely to himself. His advertisement proved again the premise that *when you use surprise, you'll gain benefits that are out of all proportion to the efforts expended.*

˙ *POINTS TO REMEMBER*

Benefits you'll gain

1. Use proper security and you'll benefit by not tipping your hand to your competitor.
2. Your proper use of security will keep your competitor from taking you by surprise.
3. Keep your plans and your actions properly secured in secrecy and you'll be able to take your opponent by complete surprise.
4. When you use surprise, you'll gain benefits that are all out of proportion to the efforts expended.

Security techniques

1. Consider all company business as strictly confidential.
2. Never discuss business problems outside your office—not even with your wife.
3. Never brag about your business successes to anyone.
4. Guard your company secrets as closely as you would your daughter's morals.
5. Never let employment agencies know all the details of specific jobs in your company.
6. Don't leave copies of your notes and other company documents lying around.

7. Lock all desks and file cabinets when not in use and when you go home at night.
8. Destroy all paper waste daily—*especially carbon paper.*
9. Don't reveal actual projects that are still in the developmental stages at a trade show, a fair, etc.
10. Operate on a need to know basis. Plug all possible sources of information leaks.

Tactics you can use to achieve surprise

1. Surprise is one of the most effective and powerful weapons you can use in your campaign to achieve power with people.
2. Success in using surprise depends upon concealing your true intentions and upon your speed of execution.
3. Surprise can be attained by using originality, audacity, speed, and secrecy.
4. The use of surprise will bring you results that are all out of proportion to the efforts expended.

8

How to Use a Power Play That Never Fails

I'd like to start right off here by making a very strong statement. This power play will work every time. It never fails; there are no exceptions. Out of every 100 times at bat, you'll get 100 hits! It'll work on rebellious teen-agers, nagging wives, wandering husbands, stubborn employees, dissatisfied customers, or hardened criminals.

Now I'd like to give you a list of those specific advantages and benefits that will be yours when you use this power play that never fails. This time I'll just list them for you. I don't think it'll be necessary to go over them in detail; they're quite self-explanatory, I'm sure.

BENEFITS YOU'LL GAIN FROM THIS POWER PLAY

1. You'll gain many, many true friends.
2. You'll convert your enemies into friends.
3. People will admire you and respect you.

4. People will do what you want them to do.

5. You'll have power with people that works like magic.

Now back in Chapter 2 I told you about the nine subconscious desires that every person has. And at that time I pointed out that one person's most dominant desire is not necessarily the same as another person's. I also mentioned that you should make every possible effort to find out what a person wants above all else in life so that you can help him get it. And those instructions still hold true.

However, I also want to say this right here. If you're having a hard time figuring out what a person's most dominant desire is, you can always fall back on his desire for ego-gratification—his desire to be important. You'll never make a mistake by fulfilling that big basic need of his.

I know this to be true for I have never in all my life met a single person who did not want to be important in some way. And I have never met a person I could not swing to my way of thinking when I gave him that feeling of importance he wanted so much. Even that rare individual who thinks that he does not want to be important still insists that you listen and pay attention to that point of view. He still insists on being heard! As one author once said, "You really can't understand humility until you've read my book. It's the last word on the subject!"

So every single person in this whole wide world wants the attention of other people, whether he wants to admit that or not. He wants to be listened to; he wants to be heard. He has a deep and burning desire—yes, even an insatiable craving—to be important, to be great, to be famous.

Just for instance, take the fellow who's never had his picture in the paper since his high school graduation. Why, he'll jump at the chance when you offer it to him. That's why people always wave when the TV camera swings their way. It's an automatic reaction to gain attention.

Use a man's basic desire
to be important

I'm saying here, then, that you can always benefit from a man's desire to be important. You'll never go wrong by doing your utmost to fulfill that basic need of his. And in a great many instances, you'll find that a feeling of importance is that person's most dominant desire anyway. So make a man important. Gratify his ego. Make that a habit; make it a routine for every person you deal with.

Now I feel certain you've heard this idea before. No doubt you've read many times that people want to be important, that they need to be recognized, that they demand to be heard. And I'm sure you've also heard that if you know how to fulfill this tremendous desire for importance that everyone has, you can write your own ticket. *You can't help but succeed*—or so you've been told.

Well, I'll tell you something else here, too. I'd be willing to bet you right now that you don't know how to go about giving a person that recognition that he wants so badly. I'll bet you still don't know precisely how to make a man feel important.

And just knowing that a man wants importance is not enough. You must show him how he can get it. You must know how to give him what he wants before you can ever hope to gain power with him so you can get what you want, too.

TO GIVE A MAN
A FEELING OF IMPORTANCE

Give your whole-hearted attention to the other person. You can do that if you'll follow these steps:

1. Become genuinely interested in other people.
2. Always *think* in terms of what the other man wants.
3. Learn to listen with everything you've got.
4. Practice patience.

5. Never take another person for granted.
6. Be concerned.

When you practice these techniques to give another person your whole-hearted attention, you'll give him a deep feeling of importance that he's never had before. And I can assure you that you'll have him completely under your control when you use them. So now let's take a look at them from the top down again, this time in detail. First, let me show you some of the good things that can come your way when you do.

Give your whole-hearted attention to the other person

Psychologists, psychiatrists, ministers, business and management consultants, criminologists, marriage counselors, all have come to one simple conclusion in this art of dealing with people: that is that if you really want to get results from them, you must master the art of giving your whole-hearted attention to the other person. It's the only way you can be sure of gaining power with people so you can get what you want, too.

Why is this so? Well, it's simple, really. Our actions to attract another person's attention are simply the outward manifestations of our inner desires for importance. We yearn for attention. We want our ideas and our opinions to be heard. The desire for attention is present in all of us. If you think not, let me ask you if you've ever been snubbed by a haughty waiter, left standing on a corner by an independent bus driver, or completely ignored by some store clerk. You know exactly what I'm driving at now, don't you?

Even the richest people need to be important   Money alone won't give a person that feeling of importance he needs so badly. The richest people in the world still want recognition and need attention. Let me show you what I mean.

Back in Chapter 3, I told you about Paul Meyer, the president and founder of Success Motivation Institute in Waco, Texas. But I didn't tell you how he got his ideas for SMI in the first place. Success Motivation Institute exists today because some millionaires in Jacksonville, Florida, still needed something their money couldn't buy for them. *They needed to be important to someone else; they needed attention.*

Now before Mr. Meyer founded SMI, he was selling insurance in Florida. In fact, he made his first million doing that even before he was 27. And it was while he was in Florida that the flash of inspiration came to him at a yacht basin in Jacksonville. It was this sudden insight that was to grow into a brand-new and different idea: selling success—and SMI.

Mr. Meyer reasoned that anyone who had a yacht must also have some good ideas on how to become successful. Jotting down the license numbers of those yacht club Cadillacs, he traced the owners, then asked each one of them, sincerely and honestly, to what they attributed their success.

These people were impressed by Mr. Meyer's sincere approach, and they answered his questions without hesitation. Mr. Meyer right there was practicing the method you're learning now—*giving his whole-hearted attention to the other person.* And when he did that, he got what he wanted, too.

In spite of all their money, these rich people still craved attention Hard to understand, perhaps, but still true. These people had Cadillacs, yachts, mansions, and everything else that money could buy. *But they still craved attention. They still needed ego-gratification.*

And Mr. Meyer got the information he wanted from them by fulfilling their need for attention. He took their answers, sifted them, expanded them, and reassembled them along with some original concepts of his own. The net result of all these ideas became his own personal "Blueprint for Success," and the foundation for Success Motivation Institute's first course.

Today, SMI is one of Waco's leading and fastest growing industries. And it exists primarily because Mr. Meyer knew how to apply the power play that never fails. He knew how to give his whole-hearted attention to the other person. And by doing this, Mr. Meyer also gained a benefit that I didn't even mention back in the beginning of this chapter: *Money*.

Mr. Meyer gained power with people—he got what he wanted— by paying attention to the other person. And you can do the same. If you don't know anywhere else to start, then start at home. You say you still don't know how? Then let me show you; it's really quite simple.

Go out of your way to pay attention to your wife   You don't have to send her flowers or candy every other day to show her how much you appreciate her. My method costs you absolutely nothing and it's even more effective. I know a couple who've been happily married for nearly 30 years now, and I know for a fact this man doesn't give his wife any presents except on her birthday, their anniversary, and Christmas!

"What's your secret, Bill?" I asked him.

"Very simple, Jim," he said. "First of all, I pay attention to her. I always let her know by my actions that I know she's around. I still say *please* and *thank you* even after all these years. So does she; sort of builds a mutual respect between us. And I never once get up from the table without saying, 'Thanks, honey; that was a terrific meal,' or 'Thanks a lot, dear; you're really a wonderful cook.'

"Or when we pass each other in the house, I reach out and just brush her hand gently. Or I bring her a glass of water when she's sitting down watching TV in the evening. Or a cup of tea in the afternoon when she's sewing or knitting. What if she doesn't want it? What if she's not thirsty? Don't worry about that. She'll drink it anyway just to show her appreciation for my giving my whole-hearted attention to her."

I know these might sound like tiny inconsequential things to do at first. They might not seem like much, but just as Bill says, they serve as proof positive to your wife that you still love her and that you still appreciate her. So if you want to maintain a harmonious relationship and a pleasant atmosphere in your home, then all you need to do is give your whole-hearted attention to your wife, too. You'll be mighty happy when you do. For when you do these little things for her, your benefits will multiply for you, too. I'll guarantee that you'll never want for a clean shirt, you'll never put on a pair of unpressed pants, or you'll never sit down to a cold supper. Your wife will love those *little inconsequential* extras and she'll want to make sure that you keep them coming.

It'll work on your children, too   It doesn't take a lot of extra effort to give some special attention to your children, too. Ask them to play with you. Perhaps a game of billiards, cards, chess, checkers, monopoly—whatever you've got in the house. Even a Ouija board can be a lot of fun. (Larry, my youngest son, and I battle it out with the cribbage board in front of the fireplace on many a stormy winter night. In the summer, you have to get in line to play ping-pong in our garage!)

So play with your children; pay attention to them. It'll improve your entire family relationship. Your kids will love you for it, too. And you'll feel better toward them, A good healthy game of table tennis in the garage with your teen-age son will do more to reduce that generation gap than any lecture you give him in the back bedroom.

Become genuinely interested in other people

There is no faster way on earth of driving people away from you than by constantly talking about yourself and your own accomplishments. Not even your best friend can put up with never-ending stories of how important you are. Even he will reach the limits of his endurance eventually.

If you believe that you can win friends and gain power with people by getting them interested in you and your affairs, then I must tell you quite bluntly: you are wrong. The only way you can win lasting friends and gain power with people is to become truly interested in them and in their problems.

It is the person who has no interest in his fellow human being and his problems who always has the greatest difficulties in life and ends up causing the most harm to others. That person will always fail until he changes his basic attitude toward people. If you're in that rut, there are two giant steps you can take to get out of it so you can become genuinely interested in others—

    1. Forget yourself completely.
    2. *Think* that other people are important.

Forget yourself completely   All of us are self-centered most of the time. To me—the world revolves around me. But as far as you are concerned—it revolves around you. Most of us are always busy trying to impress someone else. We are constantly seeking the spotlight. We continually want to be in the center of the stage. Most of our waking moments are spent in trying to gain status of some sort.

But if you really want to attain power with people, you must forget yourself completely. And you can do that in the service of others. If you want to better understand people and win their hearts and their support, then you must be willing to help them solve their problems. You must offer to help them in any way that you can.

To be able to do this with sincerity means that you'll have to place more emphasis on their problems than on your own. And you'll need an attitude of complete unselfishness to do that.

I do know this for sure. If you are sincere, if you are genuinely interested in other people and in helping them, you will never run out of work. I guarantee that the willingness of people to accept your help will always far outrun your own willingness and your ability to help them. And when you do, you will always gain power with people. After all, that's what you're really after now, isn't it?

Christ used only one sentence to say what I've been trying to say for several paragraphs here. He said, "Whosoever will save his life (unto himself) will lose it: but whosoever will lose his life (in the service of others) the same shall save it." (The parentheses are mine.)

Think that other people are important   Christ also said in effect, "Believe that you have got it and you shall have it." In other words, all you have to do to think that other people are important is just to pretend that they are, and they will be.

Simply tell yourself once and for all that other people and their problems are much more important than you and your problems are. When you adopt this attitude, it'll come through clear as a bell to the other fellow. You won't have to put on a phony false face and butter him up to make it work.

With this new approach you can stop looking for gimmicks to make the other man feel important. You won't need any, for you've put your dealings with other people on a firm, sound, sincere, and honest basis. Sincerity and honesty are better than a gimmick every day of the week, for you can't make the other person feel important if down deep inside you really feel he's a worthless nobody. The beauty of this is that you no longer have to participate in the *games people play* to impress each other. All you have to do to make it work is just *think* that the other person is important. Pretend that it is so— and it will be so. Do the thing and you will have the power to do it.

Always think *in terms of* what the other man wants

Many people will tell you that the road to a man's heart is by talking to him about the things that interest him most. But that's not enough. That's only using a gimmick to get what you want out of him. It won't work that way and here's why.

A good number of years ago I studied Japanese at the Army Language School in Monterey, California. I really worked hard at it for my next assignment was to be in Japan with the Army Intelligence Corps. So I bought a tape recorder and spent many hours every week outside the classroom listening and repeating those strange new words and phrases over and over again. You see, I wasn't interested in learning how to speak the language like a foreigner; I wanted to be able to speak it like a native. But I still wasn't satisfied in spite of all my extra efforts. I wasn't sure that I was making enough progress so I asked my instructor about it.

"Keep right on studying," Mr. Matsumoto said. "You're doing fine. It takes a long time to really learn a foreign language. You yourself will know when you're making progress; I won't have to tell you. The day that you start *thinking in Japanese,* that's the day you're close to mastering the language!"

The same thing is true in your relationships with other people. When the day comes that you start *thinking* solely in terms of what the other fellow wants, that's the day that you're close to mastering the art of power with people.

Learn to listen
with everything you've got

I know of no quicker way to insult a person or to hurt his feelings than to brush him off or turn away when he's trying to tell you something. How many times have you been right in the middle of a good story only to have one of your listeners turn away or interrupt you and start talking on a brand-new subject? You'd have loved to strangle that individual with your bare hands, right? Even children feel the same way when their parents brush them aside, ignore them, or pay no attention whatever to their problems. And if children feel that way, what reason do you have to believe that grownups don't react in the same manner?

"You've got to give your child more than board and room," says Doctor Daniel Post, Director of the Children's Guidance Clinic in Phoenix, Arizona. "I hear the same complaint over and over from upset parents. Time and again they say to me, 'But Doctor, I just don't understand what's wrong with our son. Why should he want to steal or leave home? We give him everything he wants!'

"They give him everything except the two most important things of all: *love* and *attention.* When you talk to the youngster, it's a completely different story. 'My parents never pay any attention to me.

My dad never listens to what I have to say. He never even looks at me when I talk to him. My mother's always yelling about my long hair or my dirty jeans or why I don't wear socks, but she never listens to me either! That's all I ask 'em to do; just listen to what I've got to say for a change. Holy cow—I'm important, too!' "

Learning to listen to the other person with everything you've got means putting aside your own interests, your own pleasures, and your own preoccupations, at least temporarily. For those few moments of time it means that you must concentrate 100 percent on what the other person is saying. You must focus all your attention on him. You must listen to him with all the intensity and awareness that you can command.

Learn to listen between the lines   A lot of times you can learn more by what the other person doesn't say than by what he does. *So learn to listen between the lines.* Just because he didn't say that he doesn't want to do it your way isn't any sign that he does.

The speaker doesn't always put everything he's thinking into words for you. Watch for the changing tone and volume of his voice. Sometimes you will find a meaning that's in direct contrast to his spoken words. And watch his facial expression, his mannerisms, his gestures, the movements of his body. To be a good listener and to listen with everything you've got means you'll have to use your eyes as well as your ears.

Just listening can turn an angry employee into a satisfied one "My job is to help maintain a harmonious relationship between labor and management," says George Watson, industrial relations manager for one of Ford's assembly plants. "And I do that primarily just by listening to what the other fellow has to say. For instance, if I happen to have an angry employee in my office, here's how I handle him.

"First of all, I listen to his story from beginning to end without ever saying a single word. I don't interrupt him—not even once. I let him get it all off his chest. That's the first thing he wants. He wants someone who'll listen patiently to him; someone who'll lend him a sympathetic ear.

"Next, when he's through talking, I'll agree with him, even if I don't! I tell him I understand exactly how he feels about this, and that if I were in his position, I'd no doubt look at it the same way he does.

"Now I've taken a lot of the fire out of him already by first listening to him, and then—by agreeing with him. You know he wasn't prepared for that kind of reception. Now I'll add the finishing touches by asking him what he wants me to do about it!

"You know he wasn't prepared for that either. Ninety-nine times out of a hundred, an industrial relations man will tell an employee what he's going to do for him. A lot of customer service departments handle complaints the same way. Not me; I can't win his support that way. So I don't tell him what I'm going to do for him at all. I ask him what he wants me to do for him.

"And that's a completely new twist to most people. I've had men look at me in astonishment and say, 'Gee, Mr. Watson, I really don't know. Nothing, I guess. I just wanted someone to listen to my side of the story and see it from my point of view for a change. You've done that so I guess that's all that needs to be done. I'm satisfied; you've helped me.'

"So they leave, completely happy with the answer I didn't give them. You see, they supplied their own answer. All they wanted was some attention and someone to listen to their story. I gave them what they wanted."

So George has gained power with people just by listening to them. He's gained their confidence by giving them his whole-hearted attention. You know, many a doctor earns his fee by furnishing a sympathetic ear to a patient who wants nothing more than a little attention. And you can gain power with people by doing exactly the same thing.

Practice patience

This is an attribute with which I have never been abundantly blessed, I must confess. Patience has never been one of my better virtues. It has taken me a long time and a lot of effort to cultivate this quality, and, although I'm a long, long way from attaining perfection in it, I can claim to at least having made some progress.

One of the best ways to practice patience is not to criticize and offer snap judgments. It's always better to sleep on it first before you offer an opinion, especially if it's one that could shoot the other person down in flames. And many times patience is a question of waiting, watching, listening, standing by silently until the person you're paying this close attention to works out the answer to his own problem.

I do make it a definite point never to criticize another individual. I have enough defects of my own to worry about without taking someone else's inventory, too. However, let me be quick to point out that my hesitancy to criticize does not prevent me from taking constructive disciplinary action when it's needed. Remember that discipline is just another form of attention.

Always make allowances for inexperience   Everybody has to learn. There has to be the first time for everything. A twenty-game winner in pro ball doesn't get that way overnight. He spent hundreds of hours throwing at a target first. Winning quarterbacks and professional golfers come up the same hard way. Every top professional had to start his career somewhere as an amateur. He has to gain experience first.

So don't criticize a man and cut him down when he's brand-new and he's honestly trying to do a decent job for you. Would you criticize the bride and groom if they made a mistake during their first wedding ceremony? Even the minister who asked, "Who gives this bride away?" didn't lose his decorum when the nervous father answered, "Her mother, her father, and I do!" After all, this small mistake didn't prevent the bride and groom from becoming man and wife, so no real harm was done.

Most mistakes are like that. They're small. It's only the sharp tongue of the critic that turns them into disasters!

Sober alcoholics are the most patient people on this earth   In that great nameless and faceless society known as Alcoholics Anonymous I have seen more examples of how to practice patience than anywhere else. I have seen wives (and husbands) of alcoholics participate in the Al-Anon part of it long before their husbands (and wives) ever got sober on the A.A. program. Al-Anon is the dry part of Alcoholics Anonymous. It is a fellowship of the non-drinking wives and husbands of members (or potential members) of A.A. I suppose Alcoholics Anonymous—the former problem drinkers—might be thought of as the wet half.   .

In Al-Anon, the members learn what an alcoholic is and what makes him tick. They also learn never to harp on an alcoholic's condition. They find out that it doesn't help one bit to lecture or preach or threaten or pour the bottle down the sink. And above all, they learn to pray, to practice patience, and just to wait.

In the Alcoholics Anonymous part of the program, the same understanding patience is the house rule. If a fellow has been sober for a while and then slips off the program, goes out and gets drunk again, no criticism is ever levied at him when he comes staggering back. There are no cries of "You should have known better," and he is not black-balled or barred from membership. If he says he's still a member of A.A., then he's still a member of A.A., and that's all there is to it.

Never take another person for granted

One of the fastest ways to lose power with people is to take another person for granted. A lot of people don't realize that it takes as much work to hang onto a customer as it does to get him in the first place.

For example, a girl goes all out to get her man. She primps, perfumes, dresses up, looks like a doll, and really butters him up. Then she marries him, and she sits down and lets herself go completely to pot. In less than five years she gains 40 pounds, gets slovenly, and could care less. After all, she's captured her husband. As far as she's concerned, the hunt is over. And then she wonders why he becomes unfaithful and ends up with a mistress!

And men are just as guilty. He works his head off to catch the girl. He plays the part of the perfect gentleman until the preacher says, "I now pronounce you man and wife." Then he figures his courting days are over and he assumes the attitude of the Tennessee mountaineer who says, "The best way to keep your wife is to keep her pregnant, barefooted, and chained to the bed!" From then on he takes her for granted. She's just another stick of furniture to him; that is, until she files for divorce charging him with cruelty and neglect.

Business men make the same mistake   I traded at a particular filling station for several years and then I suddenly stopped. But before I took my business to another service station, I went in and told the owner quite frankly and honestly why he was losing me as a customer.

"Before I became a regular customer of yours, you bent over backward to give me service, Max," I said. "But once you thought you had me hooked for good, you took me for granted from then on, and you concentrated only on getting more new customers.

"You stopped checking my tires and my battery. You even forgot to clean my windshield several times because you were so anxious to get to the other fellow. You left my gas tank cap on the pump at least three times and when I got upset and complained about it, you tried to laugh it off as a big joke. But it wasn't so funny to me, especially when I didn't find out it was missing until I was 200 miles away in Kansas City and had to buy a new one!

"And more than once when I've left my car in the morning to be greased and have the oil changed, I've come back in the afternoon when you said it would be ready only to find that you'd done nothing at all because you were too busy putting other customers' cars up on the grease rack ahead of mine!

"And perhaps you remember the time I mentioned it and you tried to sluff it off by saying, 'Oh, I didn't think you'd mind coming back tomorrow, Jim. After all, you don't really work. You just sit at home all day and write!' "

And so that ended our conversation. I changed gas stations. You see, Max forgot that *the best way to get new customers is to pay attention to the old ones*. Then the old customers will bring the new ones in. In fact, there's really no other way to do it, and you ought to remember that, I think.

Be concerned

You know, you can't make the preceding steps work unless you really care about people. You must be deeply concerned about them. Your heart must be filled with compassion toward others.

The devil pays a lot of attention to people. He's deeply interested in them. But he has no love, no compassion, and no deep concern for them. That's why in the long run he'll fail, just as did Genghis Khan, Napoleon, Hitler, Mussolini, and Stalin. Dictators always do.

There just isn't any use for you to pay attention to the other person unless you honestly care about him, unless you are really willing to share his pains, and help him solve his problems. To be concerned about the other man is the basic foundation for all deep and lasting human relationships. It is the heart of all friendship and a real key to power with people.

POINTS TO REMEMBER

If you want to use a power play that never fails, then—*Give Your Whole-Hearted Attention to the Other Person.* You can do that if you'll follow these six steps:

1. Become genuinely interested in other people.
2. Always *think* in terms of what the other man wants.
3. Learn to listen with everything you've got.
4. Practice patience.
5. Never take another person for granted.
6. Be concerned.

When you do these things. . . .

You'll gain these benefits

1. You'll gain many, many true friends.
2. You'll convert your enemies into friends.
3. People will respect you and admire you.
4. People will do what you want them to do.
5. You'll have power with people that works like magic.

How to Develop
Your Follow Through

The young bowler seemed to do everything just right in his approach. He stepped off with the proper foot. He did not drift from side to side on his way to the foul line. Nor did his eyes stray from his target. He released the ball smoothly and watched it roll down the alley to break smartly into the 1-3 pocket just at the right moment—only to leave the 5 pin standing! What happened? What went wrong?

"Your ball had no strength," his instructor said. "It had no power because you quit before the job was done. *You had no follow through!*"

And the same remark is made every day of the week by golf instructors, baseball and football coaches, managers and foremen in industry, sales managers in business, officers in the army, etc.

"You failed because you didn't follow through!"

BENEFITS YOU'LL GAIN
WHEN YOU DEVELOP YOUR FOLLOW THROUGH

You can exploit your initial success

In war, victory will go to the commander who has the ability and the foresight to follow up his advantage. Once the line has been breached, once the enemy turns toward the rear, the opportunity has come to completely eliminate him. A confused enemy in disorganized retreat is an easy mark for a swift and determined pursuit.

In business the same idea holds true. When you've sold him the suit, don't stop there. Follow up and sell him the shoes, socks, tie, shirt, and hat to go with it!

The biggest profits in the automobile industry aren't made when the car is sold. They're made when the sharp salesman gets the buyer to add on all those plush optional extras, from the stereo tape player to the push button controlled electric antenna.

No matter what business you're in or how you want to apply this idea of following through, you can exploit your initial success when you follow this simple rule: *Follow up your victory with the utmost energy.*

You'll insure continued success

If you've developed your resources and made ready for the long haul ahead, you'll have sufficient reserve strength to follow up and insure continued success. Today, young musical groups come and go constantly. Out of every 100, only one or two will still be around a year after they've started. Why? Well, as Johnny Carson on the Tonight Show has said, in effect, "They don't have more than a few numbers that they can do for the public. They sound terrific for the first four or five songs, but after that, they're dead. They can't get past the second encore!"

You can avoid that death trap if you'll develop your follow through to insure your own continued success. And you can do this easily if you'll follow these

TECHNIQUES YOU CAN USE
TO DEVELOP YOUR FOLLOW THROUGH

1. Make the extra effort.
2. Make yourself needed.

3. Go the extra mile.
4. Give 'em more than the other fellow.
5. Always give 'em more than they pay for.
6. Supervise the corrective action.
7. Be persistent; don't give up.

Make the extra effort

The man who earns $50,000 a year is not five times as smart as the man who earns $10,000. Far from it. In fact, he's probably just a tiny bit smarter. A little increase in knowledge can bring about a tremendous increase in salary. The fifty thousand dollar a year man has to be only a bit better than the other fellow. All he needs is the slightest edge and he usually gets that edge by making the extra effort that it takes to win.

Look at Sears Roebuck for instance. At the end of 1964 they held the number two spot for total volume of retail sales. They were the second largest retailer in all the world. The Great Atlantic and Pacific Tea Company was the biggest. But Sears was not satisfied to hold down second place. They wanted to be the biggest retailer in the world and by the end of 1965, they were. How did they reach the number one spot and beat out the Great A & P?

They used many procedures, of course, but here are just a few of their main ones. One of the most dependable standbys is the method of selling the socks, shoes, tie, and shirt to go with the suit. Another highly effective method is that of guaranteeing satisfaction or your money back without ever a single argument or question. Still another is the motto of "No Money Down" on anything you buy at Sears. They also have the best customer follow-up in the business. When they say, "Sears Services What It Sells," they mean just that—they do!

Sears has also learned the art of telephone selling. My wife answers the phone at least once a week to find them on the other end of the line calling her attention to some special sale or bargain to be had in their store. Although courteous to the core, Sears is still the most aggressive telephone seller in all the world. And they never give up. They always follow through. Once your name is established as a customer, they'll call you until the day you die—and even the day after to sell your widow the flowers for your funeral!

But above all, Sears makes the extra effort to get every single employee of theirs to go all-out to render service to the customer. To make sure each employee does just that, they've placed a card near every cash register, under the glass on every executive's desk, and on every vacant wall that can be found. It reads like this:

> A corporation may spread itself over the entire world, may employ a hundred thousand men, but the average person will usually form his judgment of it through his contact with one individual. If this person is rude or inefficient, it will take a lot of kindness and efficiency to overcome a bad impression. Every member of an organization who, in any capacity, comes in contact with the public is a salesman and the impression he makes is an advertisement, good or bad.

So if you've wondered in the past how Sears got to be as big as it is, now you know. They make the extra effort it takes to get that way. And you can do the same thing, too. Just shift yourself into overdrive and follow through. One or two out of every hundred will make that extra effort that it takes to go clear to the top. No reason why it shouldn't be you.

Make yourself needed

Knowing your job is one of the best ways of making yourself needed by your boss. Even if you have serious personality flaws, they'll often be overlooked as long as you can do your job better than anyone else can do it. You might even be thought to be a non-conformist and a queer duck in some ways, but just as long as you're really needed and wanted, no problem.

It's comparatively easy to get a position today. But once you go to work, it's up to you to prove that you can really manage your job. You know that your boss will follow up on your activities to see how you're doing until he's well satisfied that you can handle things on your own.

So become an expert in your own specific field. Be willing to share your knowledge with others and your reputation for being needed will grow. People will look to you for the answers. And that's good.

Not every clerk wants to become an executive. Not every draftsman wants to become an engineer. Some salesmen don't want to become the sales manager. Many a sergeant has turned down an officer's commission. A lot of people are perfectly content with the jobs they have and where they are right now. And that's perfectly all right if that's what they want. But I assume you want something more for yourself. And no matter what you're doing right now, I know you can be happier by doing your job better and be earning recognition for doing it, too.

Let's just pretend that you're a salesman. The best way you can follow through on your job is to increase your knowledge of your own product and the products of your company's competitors. You should acquaint yourself thoroughly with company policy; the history of the industry; the whole manufacturing process of your product from beginning to end; your company's research and development program; its marketing operations; your own customers' peculiar problems. Do these things and you'll make yourself more valuable to your company. You'll make yourself needed by both your boss and your customers by following through and learning everything there is to know about your job.

Gain a reputation for being dependable   Once you know your job, your next step should be to make it well known to the right people that you can always be depended upon to do that job and to do it well. About the finest reputation you can build with your superior is to have it said of you that you "get things done."

If you're going to earn that reputation with your boss, he must be able to rely upon you to carry out his orders actively, aggressively, intelligently, and willingly. Don't misunderstand me here. Your boss should not expect blind obedience from you. Dependability does not demand blind obedience. A reasonable boss will always be willing to listen to suggestions for improvement from his subordinates. If he is not, I'll wager that you'll soon be his superior!

There are six specific steps you can take to develop this quality of dependability. They are:

1. Never make excuses for failure.
2. Don't evade responsibility by passing the buck.
3. Do every job to the best of your ability, no matter what your personal beliefs are about it.
4. Be exact and meticulous about doing the details of your job.
5. Form the habit of always being on time.
6. Carry out the intent and the spirit as well as the literal meaning of any order.

Let me wrap up this idea of making yourself needed by others this way. You can improve your position, whatever it is, by making yourself needed by the people you serve. Whatever your job is today, you can find recognition and a better job waiting for you tomorrow if you'll simply make yourself needed by following through and properly preparing for it.

Go the extra mile

Just remember your basic mission—to gain power with people. If you want people to do what you want them to do, you'll simply have to accept the fact that it's going to take more effort on your part. You'll have to develop your follow through. You'll have to go the extra mile. Remember that if you want to get more, you'll have to give more—and the more you give, the more you'll get. Let me tell you about a couple of ordinary, everyday fellows who go that extra mile and how they benefit when they do:

"You've got to go out of your way for people if you want 'em to come back," says Lyle Holbrook. "Take my service station business here, for example. Why, the average guy doesn't begin to remember

when he last had his car greased or the oil changed. He's got his mind on his own business—not on my business.

"And the way I figure it, greasing his car, checking the battery, changing the oil, and rotating the tires for him is my business so I send him a card every couple of months reminding him of the last time he had his car serviced. I also send him a special card in the spring and the fall so he can remember to take care of the seasonal changes he needs.

"And my customers do appreciate it. I've had one after another come in to me and say, 'Lyle, I'm sure glad you reminded me of how long it's been since I've been in. I really did need the oil changed. Thanks for remembering me.'

"Now I'm no advertising genius, but with today's competition, I figure the guy who does a little something extra for his customer runs a lot better chance of keeping him. And my postcard reminders are that little something, extra special. They're my way of following up on my customers. My competitors don't do that, thank Heaven!"

"You don't go into the car business—you grow into it," says George Phillips, a long-time salesman with Central Dodge in Springfield, Illinois. "When the average car salesman sells a car, he hurries to get the buyer out of his sight. Maybe he's ashamed of the deal he's just made, but he acts like he never wants to see or hear from that customer again. Mister, that kind of a salesman is a flop. He floats from one car agency to another, and eventually leaves the car business. And the sooner he leaves—the better!

"If there's a single clue to success in the car business, I'd say that it can be found in these words: *Follow up—follow up—follow up!*

"I have a card file of customers that goes back for more than 20 years. Because of my friendship with their parents, I have a lot of names of sons and daughters in my customer files. But I wouldn't have those names if I hadn't followed up and kept track of every one of them.

"First of all, when a man buys a car from me, I make it a point to turn him into a close friend. I call him in a couple of days, then in a week or so, and even a month later to see if he has any questions about his new car's operation, or if he's had any problems with it. *I don't wait for him to call me; I call him.* If you wait until he calls, you know he's got a problem and then he's usually mad about it!

"I always talk to him every time he comes in to have his car serviced. On his first visit I take him back and introduce him to the service manager. I spend a few minutes with him every time he comes in to build up his confidence and trust in me.

"I want to make sure that he remembers who I am. I'll bet you anything that if you talk to any ten people you meet on the street today, even in a small town, seven of them won't even remember the name of the salesman who sold them their last car. Oh, they'll remember the name of the agency; that's easy. But they won't remember the name of the salesman. Why? Well, he's never talked to them again, that's why. In fact, he's avoided them!

"I don't want my customers to forget my name. I want to make sure that my customers remember me. After all, the average person will buy from ten to fifteen cars in his lifetime. I'd like to have him buy them all from me!

"So I make him hungry for more information. Men love to talk shop about cars, their mechanical operation—engines, horsepower, and so on. But so few of them really know enough about a car to discuss it intelligently. And a lot of so-called car salesmen don't know how either. They don't even know what's under the hood of their own product!

"I use that year or two between this new car and his next one to fill him up with facts about engine design and operation. That way he'll understand the engine improvements I'm talking about when the next model comes out. I give him tips on how to check minor mechanical points himself; how to cut down on tire wear; how to increase the life of his battery, and anything else new that comes along.

"When his car is two years old, I contact him when the new models come out. I don't send him just a piece of advertising literature with my name rubber stamped on it, either. Any old car salesman can do that!

"I've worked up a small brochure to give him some facts and figures about his old car and the new models. I show him in this folder how much he paid for his old car, the approximate depreciation, its current value, what his previous trade-in allowance was, and what work he's had done on it at our garage.

"Then I cover the mechanical differences between his car and the new models. I mention the new features, new designs, accessories, etc. I tell him all the advantages he'll gain and the benefits he'll enjoy with this new car. I make him hungry for a new model.

"And by now he has real confidence in me. He looks upon me as an old and trusted friend. And take it from me, people are real touchy about dealing with just any salesman when they're buying a new car. They're absolutely scared to death of a stranger, and I'm glad of that, for you see—I'm no longer a stranger.

"I resell 85 percent of my old customers. My repeat business is really amazing. But I get it simply by going just a little bit further than other salesmen do to follow up and give people something more in the way of personal service. And I really do benefit when they come back to me for more."

Now in both these examples I've just shown you, each man benefited by making more money for himself. They benefited by insuring continued success for themselves. Of course, making money is usually one of the primary benefits of gaining power with people. And I've never known anyone to turn this major benefit down.

These two gentlemen have also gained a lot of secondary benefits for themselves. They gained friends who respected them, trusted them, and had confidence in their judgment and their ability. They gained power with people by following up and doing something just a little bit out of the ordinary. And you can do the same. You can start by using the simple method of——

Showing your appreciation and meaning it   The sales clerk who says, "Thank you; come back again," but never looks up to see who you are, isn't expressing her appreciation at all. She sounds just like a tape recorder that's playing an endless tape over and over again. To tell the truth, I'd feel a lot better if she were a tape recorder. "Thanks" can become as meaningless an expression as "How are you?" if you don't really mean it.

Don't let yourself slip into this rut. You can avoid it if you'll just go a little bit out of your way to compliment at least three people a day. Looking for persons to compliment will help you develop an awareness of people. And looking for their good points will increase your appreciation of them. Then you can say "Thank you" and really mean it.

Always give 'em more than the other fellow

This is another technique you can use to make sure you develop your follow through to gain power with people. In Ames, Iowa, there is a little store known as "The Cookie Lady's Shop." The proprietor of this busy establishment, Mrs. Baylor, is better known throughout this bustling college town as "The Cookie Lady."

"How is it your place is always packed with customers when your competitor's store across the street is usually empty?" I asked Mrs. Baylor.

"Oh, that's an easy question to answer," she said. "I always make sure to give them more than he does. First of all, I give everybody a baker's dozen. Grown-ups get a free cup of coffee while they're waiting for me to sack up their orders. And that really brings a lot of people in here from October through April. We get some mighty cold winters here in Iowa.

"Little girls rate a kiss and a pat on the head along with a couple of my special sugar cookies; little boys get the same treatment except that I shake hands with them. Makes 'em feel like grown-up men. And everyone, big or small, young or old, rates a cheerful smile and a sincere 'Thanks a Million!' for coming in my store.

"That fellow across the street is interested only in making a sale. I'm interested in gaining a customer. That's why I always give them more than he does. That way I know they'll be back for sure. Why, some of my little sugar cookie customers have grown up on me, but they still keep coming back for more since I always give 'em more than the other fellow does."

Now Mrs. Baylor well understands people and human nature. She knows that if two storekeepers are offering people the same thing, then the one who gives 'em more than the other one does will keep them coming back to his store.

So that's exactly what she does. *She gives them more than the other fellow.* It's one of the best ways in the world of following through and making sure that customer keeps coming back to you for more. That's the secret of this technique. Simple but highly effective. Just give 'em more than the other fellow does.

Remember that the object of a person in business should not be to make just a single sale, but to make a permanent customer. In every business, it's a maxim that the first sale is always the hardest. It's like getting the first olive out of the bottle, or a girl's first kiss. After the first one—the rest will come quite easily. It is also true that after you've made your first sale your hardest work will be over. Your real profits will start when he does become a regular customer of yours and when he keeps coming back to you for more.

But don't kid yourself. Even then it's no gravy train. The second olive can get stuck in the bottle just as easily as the first one, and even the best of girls can turn fickle on you. So you simply have to keep on giving them more than the other fellow to keep them coming back to you. Another good way of developing your follow through and keep 'em coming back is to——

Always give 'em more than they pay for

There is only one place I can think of where this technique will not work. It will not hold up on Sunday morning when the preacher's sermon runs overtime. This is one place where no one wants to get more than they pay for. But other than that, there's no exception to this simple rule.

Give them twenty ounces to every pound   I watched Mervin McClenahan as he worked in his meat market talking to his customers while he wrapped their choice cuts of meat. Mervin is one of the few remaining independent butchers in the country who still makes a good living by specializing only in select cuts of meat. And what with all the serve-yourself meat departments in the supermarkets, individual, independent meat markets where you can pick out the exact steak or roast or chops that you want are becoming as rare as the blacksmith shop and the harness store.

But Mervin still earns an excellent income in his small, but highly successful, market. "How do you manage to do it?" I asked. "Especially when you sell nothing but meat?"

"I give 'em twenty ounces to every pound!" says Mervin. "Sure, those supermarkets sell meat cheaper than I do. They ought to; they buy cheaper meat! But they can't give you the personal service I can. Besides, they weigh the paper, too! And you only get to see one side of your meat. They hide the other one with that cardboard.

"I give every customer of mine the extra special touch. Everyone who comes in here is a VIP. A lot of my men customers like to come back in my big walk-in freezer and show me which porterhouse they want and how thick they want me to cut it.

"My women customers are just as important, too. Every piece of meat I sell in here is 'the best one in the house, just special for you, Mrs. Jones!' Every roast that goes over the counter was 'set back just for you, Mrs. Smith!'

"Even when I slice ham for a customer, I let her watch the scales. When I get the exact weight she asked for, I call her attention to it, and I say, 'There you are, Mrs. Brown. One pound—16 ounces. But I'll tell you what. Today I'm going to add a couple of extra slices just for you because you're such an extra special customer of mine!'

"Sure, I charge 10 cents a pound more than my competitors do. My meat is better. But my customers are happier than theirs 'cause they're getting more than they paid for. They're getting 20 ounces to every pound!"

Anybody can do it; you can do it, too   My barber uses the same system on me. Sure, my hair is getting thin on top. He's not kidding me one bit when he says, 'Looks like you've got some new growth coming in up there, Mr. Van Fleet!' That sounds real good to me. You know I'll be sitting in his barber chair long after I'm down to just wishful thinking, for he gives me much more than I paid for. He gives me a lot more than just a haircut. He restores my ego and my lost youth!

My wife goes to the same beauty shop every Friday for exactly the same reason. They give her more than she pays for there, too. "They don't just give me a hair-do and fix my nails," she says. "I could get that done just a few blocks away. But I drive clear across town to go to this one. Why? They turn me into a real sex symbol by the time they're through with me!"

Supervise the corrective action

The ideal to strive for is to do things right the first time. But since this doesn't always happen, you must be prepared to do something else. That's why I showed you how to become an expert in solving problems back in Chapter 3. Now for some reason or other a lot of executives, managers, foremen, businessmen, army officers, etc., will do a whale of a job in solving a problem. And they'll issue a proper order that's easy to understand to correct the situation. Then they'll walk away assuming that everything's going to be all right.

The next day they find that absolutely nothing has happened to change the status quo. No changes have been made. People are still making the same old mistakes. Why? Well, no one followed through to make sure that the corrective action was carried out, that's why.

How many times have you put out some instructions and come back only to find that no action had been taken? And what was the answer? What reason was given? I know it only too well and I'm sure you do, too. "But I told him to do it. It's not my fault it isn't done; I told him about it!" Wasn't that about what you heard? But just telling a man to do it isn't enough. That'll never get the job done. You must follow up and make sure that he does.

"Quality control is the industry's biggest headache," says Ken Griffin, president and general manager of Griffin Motor Home Sales, Inc., in Van Nuys, California. "Of course, this was bound to be our worst problem. It always is when an industry mushrooms overnight. And that's what happened in motor homes.

"Just a few years ago there were only two big names in the field— Winnebago and Open Road. Today, there are nearly a hundred manufacturers of quality motor homes. And just to show you how fast things can change, the number two company in sales today is slightly more than a year old!

"Most complaints arise because something wasn't done quite right at the factory. Maybe a wire wasn't hooked up on the furnace, or a washer on a water line wasn't tightened quite enough. Nine times out of ten, it's going to be some simple little thing that could've been prevented by a top notch quality control section. But the motor home field is so new, the quality control people had to learn right along with the rest of the production line.

"Things are looking up, though. We don't have near the problems there were a couple of years ago. The manufacturers are following up and getting rid of problems as they go along. Those who didn't aren't in the business any more. And I follow up on my customers here, too. I back each sale with service that's second to none. I follow through on every single one."

Just remember that issuing an order to solve the problem or to correct the situation is not enough. You must follow up and supervise that corrective action to make sure that it's done. Don't be satisfied just to start the ball rolling. Success will almost always depend upon your own willingness to follow through and check the end results. Time consuming? It sure is, but I know no other way to make sure the job is accomplished. You have no other choice; you've got to follow through.

Be persistent—don't give up

Of all the qualities required to succeed, persistence is without a doubt one of the most difficult to develop. It's easy to be full of fire and persistent about a project when everything's going OK, but it's a tough proposition to handle when it starts raining inside!

But you can use failures and setbacks to help you on the way to success if you refuse to give up. Read the biographies of great people and you'll find that each one of them was licked and down for the count more than once. It is not possible to win high level success without meeting up with opposition, hardship, and setbacks. Few are the people who can cross the river of life without getting their feet wet.

History books are full of stories of failures turned into success. Only one such was Thomas Edison who spent more than $40,000 in research and experiments before he came up with the first light bulb. And that was back in the 1870's. Think of how much money that would be today!

In recent history, President Richard M. Nixon, defeated in 1960 by President John F. Kennedy, seemed doomed to political oblivion. But he came back to win in 1968 because he was persistent. He simply refused to give up his dream of winning the presidency.

Persistence is the key that you can use to turn failure into success, defeat into victory. As I once heard it put, "Persistence is when your hands and feet keep working even though your head says it can't be done!"

To sum it up, then, let me say that to develop your follow through, you'll need to practice the first six techniques almost all the time; but the seventh technique—that of being persistent and not giving up—you will have to practice all of the time.

And it will take a persistence that President Calvin Coolidge once described in this way: "Nothing in the world can take the place of persistence. Talent will not; nothing is more common than unsuccessful men with talent. Genius will not; the world is full of educated derelicts. Persistence and determination alone are omnipotent. The slogan 'Press on!' has solved and always will solve the problems of the human race."

That's the kind of persistence you will need for that's the kind of persistence it will take.

POINTS TO REMEMBER

Benefits you'll gain
when you develop your follow through

     1. You can exploit your initial success.
     2. You'll insure continued success.

Techniques you can use
to gain the benefits

     1. Make the extra effort.
     2. Make yourself needed.
     3. Go the extra mile.
     4. Give 'em more than the other fellow.
     5. Always give 'em more than they pay for.
     6. Supervise the corrective action.
     7. Be persistent; don't give up.

10

Shore Up Your Own Defenses— Don't Let People Overpower You

Now in the last couple of chapters we talked about how to get what you want by fulfilling another person's needs and doing it better than anyone else. And that's the best way to get what you want from other people; no doubt about that. The only thing is, though, sometimes you can get so absorbed in doing that in your campaign to gain power with people, that you forget to shore up your own defenses and keep people from trying to over-power you.

The only people you really need to keep your eye on are those who try to get what they want from another person without fulfilling that person's needs. They give back nothing for what they get. And since they normally have no real personal power of their own, they try to get what they want by using the position or the status of others. In other words, they are parasites; they try to get something for nothing.

You've met some of them many times before. Perhaps you've even had lunch with one of them and been deeply embarrassed at the way he delights in making a false show of importance; the way he keeps a waitress on the run just for the apparent satisfaction of doing it. Then there's the golfer who treats his caddy or the bartender at his club the same way. Or the person who always pretends to have the ear of the old man, or the inside track with the front office, so everyone'll always be extra nice to him. He's the "you do it my way, or I'll tell the boss" kind. And, of course, people usually do handle his type with kid gloves. Who knows; he might really have an in or he could well be a spy! Then there's always the fellow who wields his company's name—and his expense account—like a club of authority. He never works for anybody; he's always associated with them.

And if people like these get just half the chance, you'll suddenly find you've become their waitress, their golf caddy, their servant. Since they have no real power of their own to sustain themselves, they'll use any means whatever to protect their position. Plenty of people can get injured in their struggle to retain their parasitic power. So in this chapter, I want to show you how to shore up your own defenses so they'll not be able to overpower you.

YOU'LL GAIN THESE BENEFITS

You'll retain command

You'll retain command of the situation, not only in name—but also in fact. Agency or borrowed power evaporates when the agency is gone. Real personal power has staying power. No one can take it from you. A real estate salesman has power to sell a client's house until the owner terminates that agency. Then his power disappears.

I once knew an army lieutenant in a reserve outfit called to active duty in World War II. He had sergeants and corporals hopping like mad until he went back to his job as elevator operator after the war. His power was dropped as he passed through the gate at the separation center, for he carried it only in his gold bars. He had no real personal power to carry the load for him in civilian life.

Now it's an old, old saying in the service that you salute the uniform—not the man. Yet I've known many officers myself in the army whom I've saluted with pleasure even when both of us were in civilian clothes because of the fine men they actually were. But their power rested in more than their leaves, their eagles, and their stars. A certain, definite, discernible real power was resident in them at all times—whether they were in or out of uniform.

Since your power with people is based on an understanding of them and what they want, yours will continue on without pause, too. You'll always retain full command of the situation because of your knowledge of what power really is.

You can turn off their play for power

You can turn their play for power off at will and gain more personal power and stature for yourself. Nothing succeeds like success and nothing defeats a man like defeat. The smallest crisis forces the borrower of power to run back to the source (his boss) for reinforcement, since he has no authority or power of his own. His slightest mistake will make him run for cover for it exposes his real weakness.

Now at first glance it might seem you should not concern yourself with people who use a false external power to gain their ends, but only with those who have a real personal power to use. But look at it this way: If that person uses his real power properly to fulfill a person's needs (and chances are he will, since he understands the meaning of power), then any transaction you have with him should normally be beneficial to you. Of course, you should deal with him with caution. That's the rule to use at all times with all people.

You'll run into both kinds in all professions and occupations. If you're buying a car, for instance, knowing which kind you're dealing with can save you a lot of headache—and money. Usually, it's the freeloader, the user of borrowed power, you really have to watch out for. They can really harm you if you don't know how to recognize them for what they really are so you can handle them properly.

You'll know how to defend yourself

When you understand how people use agency or borrowed power to gain their ends, you'll know how to defend yourself. People often defer to those with borrowed power, primarily because of their fear that they'll lose position or status if they don't. But when the situation changes, those with borrowed power are the first to go. When their source of power disappears, so do they.

So don't ingratiate or prostrate yourself to them. To do so is but to feed the dragon. The end result can be disastrous for you: a complete loss of your personal power with people.

The last benefit

These are some of the benefits you'il gain from this chapter. The last big benefit that will be yours is simply that *people won't be able to overpower you when you shore up your own defenses.*

TECHNIQUES YOU CAN USE
TO GAIN THESE BENEFITS

Analyze the reasons behind
their push for power

Keep in mind that these people who use agency or borrowed power to attain their goals want the same basic things out of life that you do. They have the same nine subconscious desires that you have. And those subconscious desires of theirs need fulfillment just the same as yours do.

What's the difference between the two of you, then? Well, you know how to get what you want by making sure the other fellow gets what he wants. The man who's using borrowed power to achieve his purposes doesn't know how to use your kind of power. He doesn't understand the principles of power with people like you do, so he has to use agency power to get what he wants. He has no other way.

So find out what he really wants; discover what he's after. If you can then help him fulfill his needs and benefit yourself at the same time by doing so, then do it. You'll have gained a friend and an ally. If you cannot, then, at least you'll know which side of the fence he's on and you can govern your own actions accordingly. But even if he doesn't respond to your overtures, you don't have to despise him; just categorize him.

Know your business and stick to it

Nine times out of ten, a person traveling on borrowed power is not an expert on anything. When the chips are down, you can force him to take cover by using your superior knowledge. The best way to gain that superior knowledge is to know your own business better than he does and then stick to it.

One of the main reasons for the continuing success of the Great Atlantic & Pacific Tea Company is that they stick to the grocery business—and only the grocery business. Their first store opened its doors in 1859. Over a hundred years later they're still going strong. In fact, they are the world's largest *food* retailer. Only Sears, Roebuck sells more than they do, and they didn't go past the A & P until late 1965 in total retail sales.

About two thousand years ago, Horace, the celebrated Roman poet, said, "I attend to the business of other people, having lost my own." Don't let that happen to you!

Your keystone to shoring up your own defenses and not letting other people overpower you is to know more about your job, your position, your business, than anyone else. Then your knowledge becomes power. When you understand that, you're approaching wisdom. No one using borrowed power can assault such an impregnable position. It's impossible for him to overpower you and win.

Radiate authority

Although some people do know their business and stick to it, their entire appearance and attitude, their manner and their actions invite attack. Of course, if nature blessed you with a handsome physique, if you're 6'3", built like Charles Atlas, and look like God's gift to women, so much the better; make good use of those gifts. But if nature didn't endow you so bountifully—don't worry about it. Did you ever stop to think that there's only 9 percent difference in height between a man 5'6" tall and one who's six feet tall? Besides, you can still radiate authority by your actions and your choice of words.

For instance, if you're the sales manager, and you're writing a manual for your salesmen to fellow, don't ask them to *try* your methods. They are to actually *use* them. They are not going to just *make an attempt* to improve—they will definitely *succeed*. The words *try* or *attempt* actually imply the possibility of failure. You should tell them that carrying out your programs and following your procedures will certainly bring them results.

And if you're the sales manager, then you must know more than your salesmen do, or you wouldn't be where you are. If you're the authority, then act like one. Talk like the authority, walk like the authority, write like an authority—in short, be the authority!

One of the more favorable things said about Christ was that "He taught them as one having authority, and not as the scribes." May the same be said about you!

Keep them on the defensive at all times

The best defense is to attack—to go on the offensive. When you do this, you'll keep the other fellow so busy covering up and trying to protect himself, he can find neither the time nor the opportunity to attack you. One of the best ways to attack him is to challenge him with "Why?"

"This supervisor over in the belt building department was really getting to me," says Mike Stone, shift supervisor in the mill department with Dayton Rubber Company's V-Belt plant.

"He'd been demoted and transferred out of the mill department for his failure to get along with the employees. In fact, I had his old job, and he was on fire to get even with anyone. I was his best target, I guess.

"In the mill department we turn out calendar rolls of rubber to use in the various building departments of the plant. The thickness has to be measured by a micrometer and the acceptable tolerance is only 2 or 3/1000 over or under. But even more than thickness is important. The density of the rubber has to be just right or a belt won't hold together on your car. It'll fly apart in no time at all.

"Well, this guy was sending back every roll of rubber I produced for him. Each day when I came to work I'd find 20 or 30 rolls—my whole previous day's production for his department—back in my area. Every roll was tagged with a green tag that meant it was unacceptable and couldn't be used in production.

"Plant production fell off, naturally, and the next thing I knew this fellow and I were standing in front of the production superintendent's desk. I was plenty scared, but luckily I'd been given a little ammunition by one of the old-timers in my department who'd seen this game played too many times before.

" 'Just ask him *why*,' he told me. 'And keep on asking him *why*. Make him tell you and the super *why* he can't use it! It's good rubber. I know it is; I made some of it!'

"Well, the way it started Pat said he couldn't use the rubber I was turning out—said he couldn't build good belts with it. Now I knew the tolerance was OK and the lab always checked the density of each batch or rubber before I ran it, and I told the production superintendent so. I also mentioned that every other department in the plant was producing belts with my rubber and that Pat was the only supervisor who'd been rejecting my stuff.

"I also said this: 'Since I don't know all the details of building belts the way Pat does, but only of making the rubber in my own department, I'd like to suggest that he tell us *why* he can't use the rubber, especially since the tolerance and the density are OK, and all the other departments are using it.

"I want to know exactly *what* is wrong with it so I can correct the mistake. I'd like to have him show us right out on the production line *how* and *why* it can't be used.

"The production superintendent agreed and now the situation was completely reversed. When we'd entered the office, I was on the defensive and Pat was on the offensive. When we left the office, it was the other way around.

"When it was all over, Pat was demoted one more time—right out the door and into the street!"

If one of your associates is pressing you badly, back him off and put him on the defensive by challenging him with *why*. Make him prove his point; make him prove he knows what he's talking about.

One of the best ways to keep him on the defensive is to answer his question with one of your own. Then follow up quickly with still another question.

In other words, use your challenge of *why* as a lead into a completely different subject. That's what Mike Stone did. When he went into the production superintendent's office, the question was why didn't Mike produce quality rubber that Pat could use in his department. When he went out of the office, the question was why wasn't Pat building any belts?

Don't fight back
unless you must to survive

Had Mike Stone allowed himself to become angry with Pat and fought back, he could have easily lost the battle and found himself in the street. But by reversing the situation through his adroit use of the question words, he remained completely aloof from the battle. Pat ended up fighting only himself and he lost.

Along this same line, I've always used to good advantage a couple of my father-in-law's favorite expressions. "Don't let someone else's inferiority overcome your superiority," and "A man is only as big as the things that make him mad." I don't know whether they're original with him or not, but I like them.

Whenever I get mad at the typewriter because the keys don't spell what I typed, or I'm irritated because I can't get down on paper what I want to say and I'd like to kick the wall or pound my fist on the desk, I remember these two sayings. And I know I'm sure bigger than any typewriter I've ever met, and surely I must be superior to a desk or a wall!

When you study human relations, one of the first things you learn is that only ruffians engage in conflict. You should, therefore, always appear unwilling to fight, even if you're dying to get into the thick of it. But if you are backed into a corner by some aggressive ladder-climber or status-seeker, be sure people around you understand that "I don't like to get into this, but since I have no other choice. . . ."

Whatever you do, don't let your emotions rise to the surface. You can easily be defeated by your own petty sullen moods or a hot flaming temper. A cool head never loses in a battle with a hot one. So be sophisticated about it; keep cool. Fight with dignity. To do this, you must——

Keep your own values in line

Even the best intentioned people can slip from their standards, their individual code of ethics, under the pressures of combat. It's hard not to hit the other fellow below the belt when you're gasping for air just after he belted you one right in the stomach.

"Even the best boss has his bad moments," says Henry Cummins, president and general manager of Cummins Diesel in Springdale, Arkansas. "Even the man who is inordinately fair in his judgment and treatment of others can be tempted to discriminate or use retaliatory measures under great stress.

"Of course, in the long run this will always produce bad results for him. In building a business, a career, or in just plain everyday dealing with people in general, you ought to keep these three principal points foremost in your mind.

"*Protect yourself.* By that I mean you must preserve your reputation and your good name. Don't let the heat of battle cause you to make permanent enemies. You can't afford one single enemy. He can come back to haunt you after you've won that single battle. And final victory is usually not determined by a single engagement.

"*Protect your group.* You should always keep the interests of your own people in mind. They might be your students in a classroom, members of a rifle company in the army, or the employees in a corporation. Whoever they are, if you're the boss, they're entitled to your protection and assistance.

"*Protect the bystanders.* Unfortunately, the innocent bystander who's minding his own business can be hurt by you in the fight. This so often happens in actual riots and mob violence. A policeman cracks his club over one innocent head and the entire force has a new enemy.

"Hurt someone and you'll not only make one new enemy; you'll also make enemies of all those who rally to his side in his support! How often I've seen that happen in management labor relations!"

In conclusion, let me recommend that you never, never engage in a clash of wills just to prove you're stronger than the other fellow. He could fool you. Remember the basic idea that you should not fight back unless you must to survive. If you stand to gain nothing by the conflict, then you ought to be on the outside acting as the referee, not engaged in battle as one of the contestants.

Challenge a power play with complete silence

Ever stub your toe on a rock and then hurt your foot even worse when you kicked it? Or raise up and hit your head on a cupboard door and then make it worse by hurting your hand when you took a swing at that offending door? Well, it happens to writers, too!

A writer friend of mine one day became so frustrated when he couldn't say exactly what he wanted to say, exactly the way he wanted to say it, that he finally rose up in disgust and walked over and belted the wall! He broke two fingers, broke the wall, and ended up with his hand in a cast for six weeks! And a writer who can't write is like a hunter without a gun.

The problem is, of course, the rock and the cupboard door are completely silent. They won't talk up and tell you how it happened. No matter how much you fume or kick or cuss, they won't talk back. And the quieter they are, the madder you become!

You can use the rock's tactics on your challenger. Simply ignore him. More cases of divorce come from lack of attention than from adultery. No one, but no one, likes to be ignored.

Inattention is one of the greatest weapons ever used to cut a man down to size. It's used by employees, associates, customers, even by people who serve you in restaurants, bars, and hotels. The dining car steward on yesterday's train has been replaced by the airline stewardess of today's airplane. These people are all experts at putting the obnoxious individuals in their place by the simple method of ignoring them.

You can do the same. Take a lesson from them. You can destroy your most belligerent opponent's attack by ignoring him. Simply pay no attention to his requests, his opinions, his commands, his threats, his wishes. Watch the moderator at the next town council meeting. He studiously avoids the harassing upstretched hand of the troublemaker, the sharpshooter, and the rabble-rouser. If he's done his preparatory work properly, he'll have shills scattered throughout the group with enough questions to take up all the time.

When the porcupine rolls up into a ball, the fox or the coyote cannot harm him. All their attacks are in vain. Finally the attacker gives up in disgust and walks away.

"I play for time by turning a deaf ear to them," says Scott Smith, Superintendent of Greene County Schools in Springfield, Missouri. "I look old enough to wear a hearing aid even though I don't need it. Got perfect hearing in both ears.

"But teachers don't know this. When they come roaring into my office complaining about some extra assignment, a heavy workload, some uncooperative teacher, or a troublesome student, they have to wait until I turn my hearing aid on.

"Course I've heard everything they've said. And pretending to need a hearing aid gives me a chance to ask them to repeat the question if I want still more time to think up my answer. And when they have to sit down, and repeat everything all over, maybe even a couple of times, it really slows them down. Takes all the steam out of them. In the meantime, I've had a chance to work out an answer to their question in my mind."

I was close to 40 before I realized that my father always used the same technique himself on everyone, including his own children and, especially, the preacher. He despised long-winded sermons and it was one way of cutting the minister's visit to our house extremely short. He got tired of yelling to make my father hear. But he always heard everything he wanted to hear, and that's for sure.

Incidentally, this is one of the oldest tricks in the spy business, but it's still highly effective in gathering information. Use it; you'll soon see.

Don't take orders
from someone outside your command line

This can be a source of tremendous friction in business, industry, the army, church, school, you name it. Wherever people are—you can have this problem because someone always likes to take over someone else's business.

This play for power takes place often in factories where department foremen are vying with each other for position. An extreme case of it happened in the same V-Belt factory where Mike Stone worked.

Belt building demands for rubber often outstripped the mill department's production capacity before their new calendars and mixing mills were installed. Bob C., the foreman in charge of automotive belt production, used to make sure his department would have plenty of material on hand for the night shift. He would come back to the plant after supper, go to the supervisor in the mill department and tell him that production orders had been changed and that he was to shift all production to the stripping and sheeting he needed until 11:00 PM. After that, he was to shift back to his regular production schedule.

And the young supervisor would follow the foreman's orders.

After all, he figured a department head was higher than a supervisor and ought to know what was going on. The point he failed to consider was that he was not under Bob C.'s jurisdiction; he was not in Bob C.'s chain of command. *And since Bob C. was not his superior, he, therefore, had no authority to give orders to anyone in the mill department.*

It took several months, a lot of chewing-out, and hard feelings between departments before matters got straightened out properly. When they did, the production superintendent posted an organizational command line chart in all departments, in the cafeteria, all rest areas, every vacant wall he could find, and issued strict instructions that failure to follow this chain of authority to the letter would result in immediate dismissal.

Keep this in mind. Many times people will be testing their own personal power, feeding their own ego, or even trying to show off and impress someone else. But a lot of times they can be testing you, too. They could have orders from the boss to find out how you respond to orders from those with no authority. If you give up and do what they ask without question, you will be thought of only as a "Yes" man. You could well be cancelling out your chances for promotion to a higher position. Think about it.

Build yourself some strong alliances

Few people make it on their own. Even Thoreau gave the pond back to the frogs. The time comes, sooner or later, when you have to have a friend, even if it's only to cover your own grave.

You may have a lot of competition in your group. If so, there'll be all the more need, then, for cooperation with others to meet that competition. If you're in business, for example, then attending trade association meetings, belonging to the Chamber of Commerce, the Rotary, Kiwanis, is just good sound strategy and common sense. Get everybody on your side you can.

You need to protect your own interests. If you're a member of some group and you don't attend their meetings regularly enough, you could well find you've been elected to some unwanted position like that of treasurer or secretary. That's how I ended up on the building and finance committee of my church. Now I make sure to go to church every Sunday to protect my vested interests!

Gene Mason, a young salesman with the Cadillac Plastic & Chemical Company, Kansas City, Kansas, built strong friendships within the plant. He was ambitious and competitive, and he knew he needed to establish strong bonds with the plant's employees as well as with his customers on the outside. Customer demands were greater than the available supply, and he wanted to make sure his orders were always filled first.

He soon became known as a "salesman you can really work with." And he moved into the sales manager's position and from there into the assistant general manager's spot in short order. Why?

"Because I built up strong alliances in the plant—that's why," says Gene. "I could get things done where other people couldn't. I knew the ropes in the plant. I knew the key people I could depend on and the ones I could get action from, when other management people in the company bogged down completely and didn't know who to turn to to get the results they wanted."

You should protect your own interests the same way. Build up strong friendships with those people in your group who really count. Pin-point those people who can help you become successful. You don't have to shine their shoes or polish the apple with them to get 'em on your side. Just make sure you fulfill their subconscious desires, remember? It's a sure-fire way of shoring up your defenses against the day when you'll really need them to help protect you from the people who are out to overpower you!

Work to win them over— not to eliminate them

An old, old cliche is "The only way to destroy an enemy is to make him your friend." Old or not, cliche or not, I can think of no better way to say it. When you convert all your enemies into friends, you can put away your gun and pick up the fishing pole instead.

A maxim of the Kennedy clan has long been this: "I will share with you the result of our common efforts, even though I won, even though I am the leader."

For this reason, the Kennedys, a highly competitive clan, are much loved by most people even though they win nearly every competition they enter.

Being congenial and helpful toward the loser is sound strategy to follow up your victory. The trick here is to convince them that they lost to a better man and then change them into allies. Don't destroy a man just because he fought and lost.

Had not the United States, through General MacArthur's wisdom and guidance, used this approach with Japan, they would be our enemy in the Orient today rather than being our staunch ally.

POINTS TO REMEMBER

Use these techniques

1. Analyze the reasons behind a person's push for power.
2. Know your business and stick to it.
3. Radiate authority.
4. Keep them on the defensive at all times.
5. Don't fight back unless you must to survive.
6. Keep your own values in line.
   a. Protect yourself.
   b. Protect your group.
   c. Protect the bystanders.
7. Challenge a power play with complete silence.
8. Don't take orders from someone outside your own command line.
9. Build yourself some strong alliances.

10. Work to gain them over to your side—not to eliminate them.

And you'll gain these benefits

1. You'll retain command of the situation, not only in name —but also in fact.
2. You can turn their power play off and gain more personal power and stature for yourself
3. When you understand how people use agency or borrowed power to gain their ends, you'll better know how to defend yourself.
4. People won't be able to overpower you when you shore up your own defenses.

11

To Gain Power with People—
Become the Greatest
in Your Field

Power with people is much like a triangle; it is a three-sided affair. One side of this power triangle has to do primarily with your activities to pin-point the right person and to gather positive intelligence information about him so you can use it to get him to do what you want. Most of the chapters in this book have been directed at that aspect of gaining power with people.

Another side of the triangle of power is concerned with your own actions to gain power with people by preventing them from gaining power over you. That viewpoint we covered in the last chapter. Much less time was devoted to it, for it is defensive in nature, and your best defense is an aggressive offense.

Now the last side of this power triangle covers the techniques you can use to gain power with people by becoming the greatest in your field. In other words, this chapter covers the actions you must direct inward on yourself to gain power with people. This side of the triangle works like a mirror. Your inward power is reflected outward on other people to influence them and to control their activities; to dominate their actions and reactions. And I can assure you that when you do become the greatest in your field, you will have power with people. It simply could not be otherwise.

Just for instance now, when you are the greatest in your field, you can set your own price for your services. A friend of mine was operated on in St. Luke's Hospital in St. Louis a few months ago. The surgeon's bill alone was a little over $5,000! Why was this surgeon able to charge and collect $5,000 for just one operation? Because he was called in from New York City to do the surgery; because he is thought to be the number one man today in his particular specialty, neuro-surgery. And finally, because his patient, this friend of mine, believed that he could render a service that no one else was capable of!

The clue to such power with people was given to us by Jesus when He said, "He who would be greatest of all must be the servant of all." Unfortunately, most people who read this simple scripture stumble over the word *servant*. They refuse to believe that a servant could be the greatest of all and gain power with people. And their ego being what it is, they refuse to cast themselves in the role of a servant, even to become the greatest of all.

But a simple matter of re-wording would make the phrase more understandable, and even more palatable, perhaps. So let me re-word that sentence for you right now so that it will read like this: *He who would be the greatest of all must serve the needs of all.* Now the sentence has become a definite key to power with people and every one of us can completely understand it.

For example, the storekeeper who serves the needs of all people better than anyone else will be the greatest of all and soon will be much more than just a storekeeper. He will control a financial empire! Marshall Field built the largest department store in the world using that principle. Sears Roebuck has become the world's biggest retailer by following that rule. And Holiday Inn has grown into the largest and most lavish motel operation in the world because of the founder's vision to give people the absolute ultimate in service!

Do you want even more examples of such success stories? Then look around you, my friend. Your own home town is full of them.

Or turn to the financial pages of your newspaper. There you'll find hundreds of corporations listed on the New York Stock Exchange because they are the best in their respective fields. And when you become the greatest in your own selected field, you'll also gain certain distinct benefits. Below are just a few of them.

BENEFITS YOU'LL GAIN
BY BECOMING THE GREATEST IN YOUR FIELD

You'll gain power with people

When you become the best there is in your chosen field, people will respect you and have confidence in you. You'll gain their willing obedience, their loyal cooperation, and their full support. People will turn to you for answers to their problems. They'll trust you and ask you for your advice and your help. You'll have power with people, and, after all, that's the name of the game!

You'll gain your own fair share of fame

You might not become president, but when you become the greatest in your field, you will become famous and well known. Just how far you want that fame to spread is entirely up to you. You can be a big frog in a little pond, or you can move on out and seek your fame and fortune on a grander scale. But if you do want to be bigger and go higher, you'll have to be even better. There might be fifty or more county attorneys in your state, but there's only one attorney general.

You'll make much money

Remember that success is not the result of making money, but that making money is the result of success. And when you become the greatest in your field, when you concentrate your entire efforts on successful achievement, financial gain will just follow naturally as night follows the day. You won't have to worry about it; it's a natural phenomenon. Just become the greatest in your field; the money will come to you as a simple matter of course.

TECHNIQUES YOU CAN USE
TO BECOME THE GREATEST IN YOUR CHOSEN FIELD

1. Use your God-given talents to do what you were meant to do.
2. Accept your limitations with good grace.
3. Acquire specialized knowledge about your own field.
4. Gain people knowledge.
5. Develop *your own* self image.
6. Understand yourself and seek self-improvement.
7. Act as if it were impossible to fail.
8. Do the thing so you will have the power to do it.
9. Develop a sense of humor; don't take yourself too seriously.

Use your God-given talents
to do what you were meant to do

How is it that one man can be a top-notch salesman and ninety-nine others are complete duds? What makes certain musicians and singers the best in their field? Why is one man a brilliant success and a hundred others abject failures? What makes the difference?

Why was Jack Benny the number one man in his profession for so many years? Why does Frank Sinatra sing with soul? How did Dwight David Eisenhower become a five-star general? How could Conrad Hilton build a string of successful hotels when many a lesser man would have fallen flat on his face? What makes Jackie Gleason the *Great Gleason?*

Because they are using their God-given talents to do what they were meant to do. They are doing what they can do best of all. Now I'm not implying that fate or destiny controls your future. Not at all.

I am simply saying that it is absolutely impossible for you to become the greatest in your field unless you are in the right field to begin with! You must be doing a work that will utilize your best talents to the fullest. How can you become the greatest unless you're doing what you really want to do; unless you're doing what you're best fitted to do? If Jackie Gleason had missed going into the entertainment field, he would probably be the character he portrays on TV most of the time—a disgruntled, frustrated, dissatisfied, fat bus-driver!

Fortunate indeed is the man who goes to work smiling because he loves his job. Fortunate is the man who goes to work because he really wants to go to work, not just because he has to earn a living. But the man who doesn't love his job isn't doing what God meant him to do. He's going through life traveling third class when he could've gone first class. He can't reach the top that way. I could give you one example after another of people who've switched professions when they were in their thirties, their forties, even their fifties.

Frank G. Slaughter, a well-known and prolific writer, was a physician and a surgeon. Cary Middlecoff, who won his fame as a golfer, was a dentist. Grandma Moses did her first painting at an age when most people are dead and buried. Faith Baldwin was a housewife with several children before she wrote her first book. Dutch Whitley, a close personal friend of mine, became a Methodist minister when he was 42 after being a dissatisfied electrical engineer for nearly twenty years. I wrote my first book when I was 46 years old!

Let me sum up this idea by saying that one of the most important steps you can ever take in your entire life is to find out what you're best suited for in the first place. And the earlier in your life that you find that out, the better. Don't try to make yourself into something for which you have no inborn talents. And don't take something that's second best or third best. Go for broke; go all the way. Pull all the stops. You know you'll never be happy doing a job that you don't like to do and one that you're not at all fitted for. Use your God-given talents to do what you were meant to do. You can become the greatest in your field when you do.

Accept your limitations with good grace

Accepting your limitations with good grace is just as important as developing your basic God-given talents. Every man who's 5 foot 6, near-sighted, and baldheaded wants to look like John Wayne or Cary Grant or whoever the current movie idol is. But no amount of wishful thinking can turn the trick for him. We can't all be movie actors or professional football and basketball players or home-run hitters.

When I was in high school I wanted to earn a letter in football the worst way. But I never tipped the scales at more than 118 pounds wet! So after three broken ribs, one bent nose, two missing teeth, and a twisted knee, I finally accepted my physical limitations and gave it all up as a bad job! Best move I ever made.

"When you accept your limitations, then you can learn to use your real talents," says David Young, a nuclear physicist at Stanford University in Palo Alto. "When I was a small boy I lived on a farm here in California. I loved the outdoors, and I spent every minute that I could exploring the wonders of nature in the hills that surrounded our valley.

"One afternoon I was walking along the top of a high ridge and I spotted a hawk in a tall tree that leaned away out to overlook our fertile acres. I saw a nest in that tree, and I felt sure that there must be some eggs in that nest. I wanted those eggs so badly, but I knew it was impossible to reach that nest without breaking the tree limb and falling down the mountainside.

"So I closed my eyes and prayed. I prayed for God to let me fly up to that nest just like the hawk so I could get those eggs. And as I prayed, I thought that I ought to show God I had some faith, too, so I flapped my arms up and down as fast as I could just like wings. I was so sure that God would hear my prayer and answer it, but, of course, nothing ever happened.

"And then the hawk flew into the air so gracefully from the nest. I was so envious. But as it flew away, a feeling of understanding came over me, young though I was, that God could not interrupt or change the orderliness of His creation so that little boys might fly.

"From then on I think I knew deep down inside of me that to be happy, one had to follow his inner guidance so that he might do that which God had given him the talent to do. And that he should also accept the limitations that had been placed upon him as exactly that—limitations—and nothing more. Only then could a person realize his true potential, do great things, and fulfill his own individual destiny!"

I, too, over the years have learned to accept my limitations. For instance, I cannot sing. I have a voice that would frighten a bull frog. Nor could I have ever been a carpenter or a cabinet maker. I am so clumsy with tools that if I so much as pick up a hammer, my wife heads for the back bedroom, shuts the door, and covers her ears.

A few years ago I ran across a small verse which has been credited to St. Francis of Assisi, although I think it has been rephrased by other great men down through the ages. It has helped me tremendously in accepting my own limitations and I think it will help you to accept yours, too. It goes like this:

> God grand me the serenity to accept
>   the things I cannot change,
> Courage to change the things I can,
> And wisdom to know the difference.

Acquire specialized knowledge

Now you may have all the natural ability it takes to become a first class doctor or lawyer, engineer or draftsman, businessman or corporation executive, but that won't be nearly enough. Especially in today's highly technical, highly scientific, computerized world will you need specialized knowledge.

"Knowledge is that acquired information which includes both your professional learning and your understanding of people," says Howard Wilson, a chemical engineer with Du Pont. "Nothing will inspire people's confidence and respect in you more quickly than your demonstration of that knowledge and your ability to put it to work to get results. You cannot conceal a lack of knowledge about your job. You cannot bluff people about that, at least, for very long."

Don't stop studying just because you've graduated from college and have your degree. You'll never live long enough to know everything there is to know about your chosen profession. A degree is only the first step in gaining specialized knowledge.

So continue to study, to read, and to research into every corner of your chosen profession. Sharpen those talents that God gave to you. Improve them at every chance you get. The more you know about your work, the better your chances are of becoming the greatest in your field and of gaining power with people.

Know your own job   Knowing your job will increase your confidence in your own abilities. No amount of motivation can move you to do well a job you don't know how to do in the first place. You might have all the native ability to become a great pianist, but you must learn to play the piano first. When you know how to do that, then repetition is your next move, for it will increase your confidence in your own abilities.

Practice makes perfect may be time-worn, but it is still true. Red Foley, one of the most beloved of all country and western entertainers, used to say, "If I miss practice one day, I can tell the difference. Two days, and my wife can tell the difference. But if I skip three days, then my entire audience knows it!" And that came from a master in the musical field.

When I was in Fort Benning, Georgia, far too many years ago, attending the Infantry Officer Candidate School, I went out every Sunday afternoon and gave close order drill to the trees. Those trees never moved, but I got over my fear by this constant practice; I gained full confidence in my abilities to march a platoon.

And I was not alone in my efforts. On Saturdays and Sundays the woods were full of young would-be 2nd lieutenants talking to the trees and bushes. No wonder people gave the name of *idiot sticks* to the crossed rifle insignia we wore!

But practice is the only way of learning your job thoroughly. It's the only way you can increase your confidence in your own abilities so you can truly become the greatest in your field. So practice, practice, and practice some more! Gain complete confidence in yourself and in your own abilities. Practice until there's not one bit of room left for improvement.

Gain people knowledge

All the specialized knowledge about a specific subject won't be enough unless you can use that information to gain power with people. A doctor must have patients, a lawyer must have clients, a businessman needs customers, and even a writer must have readers before his knowledge becomes useful and worth while. Book knowledge that is not put to work is completely useless to you.

And knowledge about how to handle people is just as important as that specialized knowledge you've gained, too. Perhaps even more so, for many "A" students flunk out in life because they don't know how to get people to do what they want them to do. I once knew a fellow with a photographic memory. He graduated with high honors from his university, but he lacked completely the ability to work with people.

Just how important knowledge about people is in attaining success was discovered by a large western university a few years ago. This university conducted a survey covering more than two thousand of its graduates. It wanted to find out who had succeeded and who had failed after ten years—and why. And that university found out that *the primary reason for failure was the inability to get along with people.* In short, an "A" student in science can easily be an "F" student in human relations.

So taking that basic fact into consideration, you might do well to make the study of power with people your primary vocation, and law, business management, industry, sales, or what have you—your secondary vocation!

Develop your own self image

In his marvelous book *Psycho-Cybernetics*,* Doctor Maxwell Maltz points out how important it is that you establish your own self image. He says that you can do nothing that is in conflict with your own self image. And that is true. It is absolutely impossible for you to gain power with people by becoming the greatest in your own field if deep down inside you really don't believe that you can become the greatest.

Your actions, your feelings, your behavior—even your innate God-given abilities—will be entirely consistent with your self image. In other words, you will act like the sort of person you conceive yourself to be. Not only that, you really cannot act in any other way, in spite of any conscious efforts, positive thinking, or use of will power on your part.

That is why it is so important that you create a successful self image. Now your self image should not copy or emulate another person to the point that you submerge your own personality in his. That's why the first two techniques, *using your own God-given talents and accepting your limitations,* are so vital in establishing your own proper self image. They allow you to become really *you* when you use them as guidelines.

You see, you as a person are not in competition with any other person simply because there is no other person on this earth who is exactly like you. Just as fingerprints differ, so do physiques and personalities. You are a specific individual; you are unique as such. You will never come this way again. You're not like any other person and no other person is exactly like you. There is only the one original; God doesn't make any carbon copies. And that is why you can develop *your own* self image by using your God-given talents as they

---

* Maxwell Maltz, *Psycho-Cybernetics* (Englewood Cliffs, N.J., Prentice-Hall, Inc., 1960).

were meant to be used and by accepting your limitations as exactly what they are—limitations, and nothing more. People are a very special and individual proposition. They don't come off the assembly lines like Fords, Chevrolets, and Plymouths.

Understand yourself
and seek self-improvement

Take it from me, you're the only person who can improve yourself; no one else can do it for you. The person who asks you for "constructive criticism" is either a liar, he's kidding himself, or a little of both. He doesn't really want you to criticize him at all. What he really means is that he wants you to praise him and tell him just how good he is. I know that's what he wants; I'm human, too, and I'm as guilty as he is about accepting "constructive criticism."

So I'm not going to waste any of our valuable time here showing you how to correct your mistakes, how to get rid of your personality defects, or how to improve any of your bad character traits. I know you don't want to hear that, and, besides, I have enough problems of my own to solve.

To tell you the truth, when it comes to self-criticism and self-recrimination, I'm not very good at that either. In fact, I'd like to suggest that you adopt my system. I never criticize myself. I never enumerate my own faults. I let my next-door neighbor do that for me; he does such a much better job of it than I could ever do myself. He's much more thorough about listing all my bad habits than I could ever hope to be.

And since I don't see the sense of both of us worrying about my mistakes, I let him fret and stew and fuss for both of us. That way *I* don't have to, and he gets all my ulcers. You can use the same procedure; I recommend it highly. Not only will it get rid of all your ulcers for you, but it's also very good for your heart.

Another reason I never criticize myself is that criticism is always based on that which is past. And the past belongs to yesterday. You see, there are two days of the week that you should never worry about if you want to become the greatest in your field. These are yesterday and tomorrow. You'll be kept busy enough just thinking about the problems of today. Here's how that works——

Yesterday   There are two days in every week about which you should not worry, two days which should be kept free from fear and apprehension. One of these days is yesterday, with its mistakes and cares, its faults and blunders, its aches and pains. Yesterday has passed forever beyond your control. All the money in the world cannot bring back yesterday. You cannot undo a single act you performed. You cannot erase a single word you said. Yesterday is gone forever beyond recall.

Tomorrow   The other day you should not worry about is tomorrow, with its possible adversities, its burdens, its large promise and perhaps its poor performance. Tomorrow is also beyond your immediate control. Tomorrow's sun will rise, either in splendor or behind a mask of clouds, but it will rise. Until it does, you have no stake in tomorrow, for it is yet unborn.

Today   This leaves only one day for you to worry about—today. Any man can fight the battles of just one day. It is only when you and I add the burden of those two awful eternities, yesterday and tomorrow, that we break down. It is not the experience of today that drives men mad. It is the remorse or the bitterness for something which happened yesterday or the dread of what tomorrow might bring. Therefore do your best to live just one day at a time.

So you see, when you seek to improve yourself, don't waste your time worrying about yesterday's mistakes or tomorrow's errors. The only time you can really improve yourself is right now, today, so do just that.

Now in addition to these two very practical methods, I do have three more reliable techniques you can use to seek self-improvement:

1. Always set the example for others to follow.
2. Learn to make sound and timely decisions.

3. Seek responsibility and take responsibility for your actions.

Always set the example for others to follow   When you become the greatest in your field, you automatically become a leader. And thus you become an example for others to follow whether you like it or not. But only by setting the example can the image of the leader be created. When you do set the example, you'll be able to motivate people to do what you want them to do.

Remember that real leaders are examples to be followed—not models to be admired. Setting the example isn't going to be an easy task. It means you'll have to develop or strengthen some of those old-fashioned personal qualities you and I used to hear about in Sunday School when we were children.

Learn to make sound and timely decisions   If you want to become the greatest in your field, you won't be able to pass the buck to anyone else. As President Truman used to say when he occupied the White House, "The buck ends here!" And you might as well accept the fact right here and now that making sound and timely decisions means you'll have to stick your neck out once in a while. But you'll never learn to improve yourself if you don't have the courage to make your own decisions and if you constantly turn to someone else for the answers all the time. Sooner or later you'll have to fly on your own if you want to become the best there is.

Seek responsibility and take responsibility for your actions   Actively seek all the responsibility and all the tough assignments you can manage to get. Accept them eagerly. You'll never improve yourself by doing only the easy things. This reminds me of the old man who prayed to God for strength and all God ever gave him were more problems to solve. But how else could God give the man more strength except by giving him more and harder problems to take care of?

When you do seek responsibility, you'll develop yourself professionally. When you accept the responsibility for your actions without trying to pass the buck, people will give you their willing obedience, their loyal cooperation, and their full support. You'll gain their respect and their confidence.

Act as if it were impossible to fail

Some time ago I happened to see a book which was supposed to contain practical advice to beginning writers by about forty or more different authors. However, most of their advice seemed to be that a beginning writer ought to take up some other profession to earn his living!

In fact, I only got about a third of the way through the book, for along about the fourteenth chapter, I read these words, "The odds against the beginning writer are about 50 thousand to one against ever being published!" And although I was not a beginning writer, I threw the book away; it was far too depressing. I should have known better than to buy such a book, anyway, for a few years before that, I had bought a book called *One Hundred and Eleven Don'ts for Writers*. I had thrown that one away, too. I just don't see any sense in reading books that tell people how to fail. I can do that well enough on my own!

In this respect, I am often reminded of the aeronautical engineers who can prove to you by aerodynamics and the laws of physics that the bumblebee can't fly. You see, they say his wing span is too small for the size and weight of his body, so scientifically speaking, it's impossible for the bumblebee to get off the ground and into the air. The trouble is, they forgot to tell the bumblebee that, so he goes flying merrily on his way to the consternation of all these brilliant scientists who say it can't be done!

One of the most frustrating situations in all the world is to be confronted with a problem that you *must* but *cannot* solve. This causes a complete loss of emotional security.

Psychologists have found that the *fear of failure* is a businessman's biggest stumbling block. And this fear of failure is not limited to businessmen alone. I think it is the biggest psychological stumbling block of every single living person. A man fears to fail because he fears ridicule, he fears the possibility of being laughed at. That's why an amateur writer will finish up his manuscript, put it in the desk drawer, and never mail it off to the publisher. When he does this, he's not running the risk of rejection and humiliation. As long as his manuscript is safe in his drawer, he can dream and pretend.

That's why unsuccessful salesmen spend so much time at coffee call or just sitting in the office talking to each other. They're afraid to get out and make a call because they're so deathly afraid of failure.

But to do something is far better than to do nothing, even if it's wrong. And all you need do is act as if it were impossible to fail. If you do stumble once in a while, just remember that a single fall doesn't label you as awkward or clumsy. Just because a boy flunks a math test doesn't mean that he's a mathematical failure. Or if a girl flunks one spelling test, that doesn't mean that she's scholastically incapable. Or if I get a manuscript returned along with a rejection slip it doesn't mean that I'm a writing failure. It only means that that one particular manuscript didn't sell at that one specific moment of time. That's all it means; that, and nothing more.

Do the thing so you will have the power to do it

Last year a robin built a nest in the tree just outside my study window. I watched the growth of this robin's family, from the eggs in the nest until the day that four little heads popped up demanding to be fed. And then one by one, the mother robin nudged her babies off into the air when the right time came.

But there was one little fellow who was so afraid that he couldn't fly. It took him nearly a week longer than the others, and finally the mother had to force him out of the nest. And when she did, he suddenly flapped his wings and flew awkwardly away. No one had taught him to fly at all. Nature had put the instinct there for him to do it. But he had to fly before he had the power to do it, for that is nature's law; her way of doing things. You must do the thing so you will have the power to do it. And if you will not do it, you will never gain the power to do it.

The same is true of people. We, too, must do the thing before we have the power to do it. Only driving will make you an excellent driver. Only actual flying will make you a pilot. Only painting will make you a painter; only writing will make you a writer. You'll never become a salesman until you make your first sale.

Develop a sense of humor— don't take yourself too seriously

When you become the greatest in your field, it's extremely easy to become so conceited and so egotistical that you can soon lose your coveted position as the greatest in your field. One of the best ways to retain your balance and walk the tight rope of success is simply not to take yourself too seriously.

A good friend of mine puts it this way. "I tried for a great many years to be successful," Jack Oatum says, "but I was never quite able to make the grade. So I finally decided that I must have the thing turned around somehow. So I decided to change my goals. I decided to become a failure, and I was a success overnight!"

But don't let Jack kid you. He's a success, an overwhelming success in the insurance business. He's just learned to keep his sense of humor; that's all.

POINTS TO REMEMBER

Use these techniques

1. Use your God-given talents to do what you were meant to do.
2. Accept your limitations with good grace.
3. Acquire specialized knowledge about your own field.
4. Gain people knowledge.
5. Develop *your own* self image.
6. Understand yourself and seek self-improvement.
7. Act as if it were impossible to fail.

8. Do the thing so you will have the power to do it.
9. Develop a sense of humor; don't take yourself too seriously.

And you'll gain these benefits

1. You'll become the greatest in your field.
2. You'll gain power with people.
3. You'll gain your own fair share of fame.
4. You'll make much money.

12

How to Add
the Professional Touch

Let us say for the purpose of illustration you have learned your lessons well. You have followed my instructions and my guidance implicitly from the initial selection of the proper target—those people who can help you become successful—right up through the last chapter in which you learned how to condition yourself for the long haul.

So now you are victorious. You have gained power with people. Whether you retain that power or not will be entirely dependent upon what you do now.

I can quickly say this: If you use your newly acquired knowledge of power with people as a whip of authority, if you use it to lord it over them, or if you attempt to add to your own feeling of self-importance by making other people feel small, you'll not last long. That's why slavery never works; you cannot control a man's mind by physical force.

But if you use your knowledge of power with people to *help others,* you'll find your position will be an easy one to maintain, for *people always need a competent leader who will help them get what they want.*

In fact, I'll even go further than that. I'll say that not only do people always *need* a leader, but also, that they always *want* a leader. The Old Testament has one example after the other of the people of Israel forcing the mantle of leadership and authority on the person of their choice.

I think the benefits of retaining power with people are so obvious that I need not discuss them. Instead, I will go at once into the methods you can use to add the professional touch—to put the frosting on your own cake.

TECHNIQUES YOU CAN USE
TO ADD THE PROFESSIONAL TOUCH

1. Go out of your way to help other people.
2. Never use your position for personal gain at someone else's expense.
3. Have respect for the dignity of every other person.
4. Never play favorites.
5. Always keep your word.
6. Above all—be sincere.

Now it would have been a lot easier for me to make that list of techniques four to five times as long as it is. My object, though, is to give you the most important ones: the specific procedures I have found through trial and error to be the most helpful to me in my 25 and more years of experience in this business of gaining power with people.

Another important point is this: I have always found that whenever I failed to use any of these techniques, or if I violated one of them, it always led to problems with people instead of power with people.

Go out of your way to help other people

I know this is an age of non-involvement, but I also know you cannot hope to gain a lasting power with people if you do not go out of your way to help them. To help someone get what he wants is the only way you can really get what you want. And even if helping that person doesn't help your pocketbook right then and there, it'll help your health, for it'll do wonders for your heart.

Love is spelled H-E-L-P!   Once upon a time there lived in the small town of Suburbia two neighbors named George and Jim. But they were not very good neighbors at all. They were at odds with each other, although neither one of them could remember just exactly why. So they lived in a constant state of bitter verbal warfare. Or they would not speak at all, although in the summer time their lawnmowers often rubbed wheels as they moved along their backyard battle lines.

Then one summer George and his wife went on a two-week vacation. At first, Jim and his wife did not even notice their absence. After all, why should they? They seldom spoke to each other, anyway, unless one of them had a specific complaint to register with the other.

But one evening just after he'd finished mowing his yard, Jim noticed how high George's grass was. It was especially obvious now that he'd mowed his own.

It would also be obvious to anyone driving by that they were not at home and that they had not been there for quite some time, Jim thought. In fact, it was an open invitation to a thief to break in, he mused. And then a sudden flash of inspiration hit him: *don't try to love your neighbor; just help him!*

"I looked at that high grass again," Jim says. "My mind rebelled just at the thought of helping someone I so thoroughly disliked. But in spite of all my efforts to blot the idea from my mind, it persisted. It just wouldn't go away. So the next morning, Saturday, I mowed his blasted lawn!

"On Sunday afternoon, George and his wife came home. Shortly after they got back, I saw him walking up and down the street. He was stopping at every house in the block.

"Finally, he knocked on my door. I opened it. He stood there staring at me, an odd and puzzled expression on his face.

" 'Jim, did you mow my lawn?' he finally asked. It was the first time he'd used my given name in a good long while. 'I've asked everyone else in the whole block. No one else mowed it. Jack says you did; did you?'

" 'Yes, George, I did,' I said, almost belligerently.

" 'Thanks,' he said. He turned sharply and walked away."

And so the ice had finally been broken for George and Jim. Oh, they're not playing golf together yet and their wives don't run back and forth every five minutes to borrow sugar or chit-chat. But they're making some progress. At least they are grinning at each other as their lawnmowers pass. They even say *Hi* once in a while.

Love your neighbor? Perhaps; but only if you spell love H-E-L-P! How can I be so sure of that? That's easy; I'm Jim!

It is impossible to give something and get nothing in return Don't make the mistake of thinking you can give nothing and get something back. By the same token, it's impossible to give something and get nothing in return.

But you should not expect to always get something back from the same person you help. A lot of times, you won't. The person you've never been able to repay, you're repaying right now when you help someone else. And the person you help right now, who can't possibly repay you, will pass your favor along to still another.

A petty, near-sighted person often refuses to give because he can't see where or how he's going to profit by so doing. Therefore, he gets nothing back because he gives nothing away. So you see, the maxim still holds true even in his case. He got back exactly what he gave away: nothing!

But the far-sighted man gives without any thought of immediate return and he profits from that. It's absolutely impossible to help someone without being helped in some way in return. Look at Pete Kendall, for instance:

How to help the other fellow sell your own product   Pete Kendall is a cookie salesman out of Des Moines who calls upon grocery stores in north-central Iowa. Now Pete's cookies are good, but they're really no better than half a dozen other brands. Yet Pete outsells his competitors all the time. How does he do that? By taking the extra time to *help a grocer sell his* (Pete's) *product.*

"A small town grocer just doesn't have the backing the big chain stores have for floor displays and advertising," Pete says. "Nor does he have the manpower to help him. If he's going to get it done, he has to do it himself, or get his wife to help him.

"Now you just don't walk into a man's place of business and tell him how to run things. Quickest way in the world to lose a customer. So I usually wait until the time is just right, like when I find a grocer right in the middle of putting up a cookie advertising display. Then I pitch right in and help him.

"I remember a specific store in Clarion, the So-Lo Market, where I helped the owner put up a display for one of my cookie competitors! Next time around, he wanted me to help him again, for he'd really done a booming business with that first display, but this time he wanted to do it with my cookies.

"Now he pushes my brand all the time, and, in return, I bring him all sorts of suggestions for displays on everything from brooms and brushes to yams and yogurt!

"All in all, in 73 of the stores I service, my cookies outsell every competing brand in the place. And just because the owners push my line instead of theirs. I haven't caught them all yet, but just give me time. I will!"

And knowing Pete as I do, I'm sure he will. Of course, he could've taken the easy way out. A lot of salesmen do. So many of them just stop, ask the grocer what he wants, write up the order, and then leave. Some even forget to say "Thanks!"

But that's not being much of a salesman. The fellow who does that is only an order-taker. Pete is the real salesman because *he's going out of his way to help the grocer sell his product.*

Don't kid yourself one bit about this first technique. There's only one way to get other people to do what you want them to do, and that's to help them get what they want while they're doing it.

So take it from me, please—you might just as well quit looking for those short-cuts to power with people right now. There just aren't any. I know; I've looked for all of them, too. Every time you think you've found one, you suddenly discover you're on a dead-end road!

Never use your position
for personal gain at someone else's expense

The person who uses his position for personal gain at another person's expense will not last forever, although I'll admit sometimes it seems like he will. But even professional politicians—Congressmen and Senators—can be eliminated by the disgusted voter. It happens every election year.

The unselfish leader always takes care of his people first   The unselfish executive places the welfare of his employees above his own. He never tries to gain what he wants at the expense of his own people. Remember that he who would be greatest of all must first be the servant of all.

A selfish executive will take care of his own comfort, his own desires, and his own personal pleasures, come what may, even if it means gaining them *at the expense of his own employees*. He puts privilege above responsibility.

Don't abuse your privileges   RHIP is a phrase common to the military. A young second lieutenant will tell you that it means *RANK Hath Its Privileges*. But a seasoned veteran will tell you that it's *RESPONSIBILITY*—not rank—that *Hath Its Privileges*.

No one will object to the extra privileges that go with your position just as long as you use your position of power to guard and protect their interests. Remember always to place the welfare of the group above your own if you want to retain power and control of that group.

The army officer who uses government transportation to get from his quarters to his place of duty, eats in a company mess without paying for it, or uses an enlisted man as a personal servant, is just as guilty as the traveling salesman who pads his expense account, or the plant manager in a corporation who uses company materials or company labor to repair his house.

All these individuals are despised, not only by their subordinates, but also by their associates as well, for their gross abuse of their privileges.

So if you're an executive, a foreman, a supervisor, a manager, an army officer, a leader of any sort—play your part to the letter. Your subordinates will expect you to. But they'll never begrudge you your title, your position, your prerogatives and your fringe benefits, just as long as you use your position to promote their interests and help them get what they want.

So if you do happen to be in a management slot, or if you expect to be in one some day, take a new fresh look at it. Consider it as a position that will allow you to *fulfill your responsibility to your superior by serving your subordinates*.

Big brother could be watching you   Every so often the perfect opportunity seems to come along to bury the knife in the boss's back; or so it seems at the time. But watch out; not only are you violating the spirit of this principle—not to use your position for personal gain at another person's expense—but you could also be walking head on into a booby trap. So be careful, there might be a Clinton Andrews in your outfit, too.

"I make it a definite point to call a department when I know its chief is on vacation or when he's just gone for the afternoon on personal business of some sort, maybe some golf, or some fishing in the gulf," says Clinton Andrews, vice-president and general manager of the Tampa, Florida, branch of Soroban Engineering, Incorporated.

"But I'm not checking on the department head although I make it sound that way to his assistant. I know where the department foremen and section chiefs are; they always clear it with me first before they leave. So I'm not spying on them. I want to see how that assistant reacts when his boss is gone.

"I ask for some trivial information just to find out how he'll respond. If he simply gets the information and recites it off to me without adding any digs about his boss's absence—fine. He's doing his job.

"Even if he says he can't find it for me, and he accepts the responsibility for not being able to locate it, rather than trying to pass the buck up to his chief, that's all right, too.

"But if he even hints that his boss was hoping I wouldn't call the department until he got back, or if he over-emphasizes the fact that his boss is *out playing golf instead of working as he should be,* or if he tells me how *he'll get the right information for me himself* immediately so *there'll be no more slip-ups* in the department, I know that man is going to bear watching.

"And not because he's so terribly efficient and so worthy of promotion and advancement, but because he's like a predatory animal that's gotten out of its cage. He could run completely wild all over the plant, no doubt about it, if we don't get him back in his cage again.

"He's probably reached his peak already. Chances are he's passed over it and he's beyond his capabilities in the job he's in right now. I feel quite certain he won't go any higher; I know I sure don't want him as my assistant. Would you?"

Did I touch a tender spot by chance? You might remember this the next time you're so terribly anxious to tell someone how dumb, how stupid, how inefficient your boss really is, and how he couldn't possibly hold down his job except that his wife and the VP's wife play bridge every Tuesday afternoon and bowl on the same team every Thursday morning in the wives' bowling league.

Be on guard; shore up your own defenses first. You could be promoting yourself right out of your own job into the street. Think about it; big brother could be watching you, too!

Have respect for the dignity of every other person

I said awhile ago that to love should be spelled H-E-L-P if you want to make sure it works. A great many times I think that *respect* could also be used in place of the word *love,* and be better understood by more people.

I may not love a person—in fact, I might not even like him—but I should at least have respect for his rights and respect for his dignity.

And one of the best ways you can show your respect for the dignity of every other person is to follow the time-worn but true cliche of *speak evil of no one.* If you can say nothing decent about someone else—then do just exactly that: *Say nothing!*

Whenever I find that someone is overly anxious to tell me all about the mistakes that Bill and Joe and Tom have made and all the bad things they've done, I know that person will be just as anxious to hurry on and tell everybody else the same things about Bill and Joe and Tom, but he'll soon be adding *Jim* to his list, too!

"There's one way to squelch evil rumors and gossip," says Tom Warren, a department foreman with Radiation Incorporated in Atlanta, Georgia. "Not long ago, we were having all sorts of friction between departments and sections in our plant.

"Whenever we went to a meeting in the production superintendent's office, you'd have thought we were in competing companies. In fact, we'd probably been politer to each other if we had've been. But you sure wouldn't have thought we were all on the same payroll working for the same company if you'd have attended one of those meetings!

"Rumors and gossip and plain filthy talk about foremen, their wives, the plant manager, and most of the top management people were floating all over the place. Department heads and foremen were accusing each other of stupidity and inefficiency, even to the point of malicious attempts to get each other fired.

"No one could seem to pin down the source of all this gossip. It was always *they* who said it. I grew to hate that vague word with a purple passion. We never could seem to find out exactly who *they* were.

"Then one day the production superintendent was back in the parts room of the company machine shop with the maintenance foreman, Bob Sweet. When they'd gone in the parts room, the main machine shop had been empty. The way it's built, you can't see into the parts room from the main shop because of the high shelving.

"They'd heard the door slam a few times, but they paid no attention until the superintendent heard the voice of the plant safety supervisor say, 'Hey, Mac, did you hear about Henry Smith's wife? I hear tell she's running all over town while her old man's at work. Who? With Ronald Berry, that's who. Why, I saw 'em the other day myself; they were coming out of the Rendezvous in broad daylight!

" 'Something else, too, Mac. I thought I ought to tell you. I heard your boss tell the super yesterday you weren't too sharp as a tool and die maker. Said you couldn't be trusted to turn out a decent piece of work unless he stood right over you and watched you every minute. That's right; that's what he said. Heard him myself!

"Say, did you hear that Helen over in inspection section is shacking up with Jeff Miller? You know, I saw Abe Burrows the other day . . . man, was he ever drunk . . . and Todd Evans told me. . . .'

"Well, right then the super knew who was at the bottom of all the plant gossip: The safety supervisor. To make it worse, he had access to every ear in the whole plant. No place was off-limits to him. And evidently he was the kind the head-shrinkers call a pathologic liar.

"We followed the superintendent's idea about how to stop him and it sure worked. It stopped him cold. Hank—that's the safety supervisor—always followed a definite pattern in making his inspections. For instance, when he left Bob Gilchrist's office, he'd always come straight to mine. So the minute he left, Bob called me and recited off word for word all the dirt Hank had told him about me.

"I met Hank at the door and accused him right out of lying about me. I slapped him right in the face with the exact story he'd just told Bob, down to the commas and the exclamation points! When he recovered from that shock and left, I called the next foreman down the line. He met Hank at the door to his office the same way.

"Well, in less than a week things were running smooth again. Hank was going from place to place in the plant, not saying a word to anybody, but doing exactly what he was being paid to do—checking plant safety.

"I don't think to this day he really knows what happened or how we got next to him. No, the boss didn't fire him. Why should he? We got the rumors and the gossip stopped and things back to normal again. That's all the boss wanted. He didn't want Hank's hide. Besides, Hank's a heck of a good safety supervisor. Really knows his job!"

Never belittle another person A man can tolerate nearly any insult, any defeat, any injury, and accept it with good grace. You can steal his wife, his job, his money, and although he won't like it—he'll probably tolerate it up to a point and still treat you like a civilized human being.

But make fun of a man, belittle him, ridicule him—especially in front of others—and you'll have made an enemy for the rest of your life. If you ridicule him and make fun of him after you've pulled one over on him, you better load your shotgun and place a guard at every window. He'll come after you for sure. Revenge, vengeance, an eye for an eye and a tooth for a tooth can be a greater driving force than even money or sex!

Don't show up another person This is merely an oblique method of belittling a man, or telling him how stupid he is. It's extremely embarrassing to an employee to have his boss show off at his expense; for instance, by doing a certain job better or faster than the employee can do it himself.

Of course, it's only right to assume the boss can do it better. Otherwise, chances are, he wouldn't be the boss. But if you are the boss, you don't need to emphasize it and prove your point that way.

It's important to a man's dignity to be able to do something well on his own. When you do his job better and faster than he can do it, you destroy his self-respect and his self-esteem. Instead of fulfilling one of his subconscious desires, you're taking it away from him.

Deal with every person as if he were your blood relative If you will approach every transaction with another person as if you were doing business with your own father or mother, or your own son, your actions will be tempered with kindness, justice, mercy, and love.

As Christ himself said, "What man is there of you, whom if his son ask bread, will he give him a stone? Or if he ask a fish, will he give him a serpent?"

I am reminded of the old father whose son had sorely grieved him time and time again. And finally a neighbor said to him, "If he were my son, I would not stand for what he does. If he were my son, I would disown him; I would give him up!

"I know you would," the old father said. "And if he were *your* son, I would give him up, too. But he is not your son; he is my son, and I will not give him up!"

Look at every person with whom you deal the same way. To do so is not a sign of weakness, but of strength. You will consolidate your position of power with people when you so do.

To wrap up this idea, let me say this. If you want to make sure you have respect for the dignity of every other person, then *treat every man like a gentleman and every woman like a lady.*

Never play favorites

When you start to make exceptions to the rule because of some personal preference, the rest of the people will immediately adopt a "don't give a damn" attitude toward you and what you want.

If you pass over a man who should've been promoted in favor of someone who's obviously not as well qualified, you're destroying your power with people. I know of nothing else that will so rapidly undermine your position as your unfairness or your partiality toward some individual or group.

Play favorites, and the unfavored hate you as much as they hate the favored one. That's how Joseph ended up in Egypt. He was his father's favorite son and he rubbed his brothers' noses in the dirt just once too often with his coat of many colors, his dreams, and his visions of power over them.

So they "sold Joseph to the Ishmaelites for twenty pieces of silver: and they brought Joseph into Egypt."

Don't allow your emotions or your private prejudices to creep into your decisions about people. You should carefully avoid any prejudices of race, creed, or color if you want to treat every one fairly and gain power with people.

Always keep your word

If you're to attain power with people, you must be as good as your word and your word must be your bond. To make sure you always keep your word, remember and use these three points:

1. Never make a promise you cannot keep.
2. Never make a decision you cannot support.
3. Never issue an order that you cannot enforce.

If you do not keep your word, that makes you, in very blunt words—*a liar*. If you're a liar, then you simply cannot be depended upon in any way; you cannot be relied on. You could be a genius, yet as a leader, you'd be completely worthless. It is an absolute impossibility to gain power with people and keep it if you do not keep your word. There have been few maxims in this book, but this is one of them.

Above all—be sincere

Don't be a hypocrite. You won't get by if you practice these first five techniques with tongue in cheek. You'll be as counterfeit as a 3 dollar bill if you do, and people can tell. You must be sincere.

The word, *charity*, means much more than just helping the poor or giving alms. Its principal meaning in the Bible is *love*. And you can't really love someone unless you are *sincere* about it.

So I could readily rephrase the first Verse of the 13th Chapter of Paul's First Letter to the Corinthians by replacing the word *charity* with *sincerity* so that it would read like this: "Though I speak with the tongues of men and of angels, and have not *sincerity,* I am become as sounding brass, or a tinkling cymbal."

In short, if you lack sincerity, you might as well forget the first five techniques for you'll also be like sounding brass or a tinkling cymbal.

POINTS TO REMEMBER

To add the professional touch— use these techniques

1. Go out of Your Way to Help Others
2. Never Use Your Position for Personal Gain at Someon Else's Expense
3. Have Respect for the Dignity of Every Other Person
4. Never Play Favorites
5. Always Keep Your Word
6. Above All, Be Sincere

I wish I could think of some extremely wise words that I could use to end this book, but about all I can think of is, "You've had the course. Now go to it; you're on your own!"